Ruchele

Ruchele

~

Sixty Years from Szatmar to Los Angeles

Rose Farkas

with Ibi Winterman

FITHIAN PRESS · SANTA BARBARA · 1998

Published by Fithian Press
A division of Daniel and Daniel, Publishers, Inc.
Post Office Box 1525
Santa Barbara, CA 93102

Design by Shannon L. Kenny

LIBRARY OF CONGRESS CATALOGING-IN-PUBLICATION DATA
Farkas, Rose, (date)
     Ruchele : sixty years from Szatmar to Los Angeles / by Rose Farkas.
        p.   cm.
     Includes bibliographical references
     ISBN 1-56474-245-8 (alk. paper)
        1. Farkas, Rose, (date). 2. Jews—Romania—Satu Mare—Biography.
3. Holocaust, Jewish (1939–1945)—Hungary—Budapest—Personal narratives.
4. Holocaust survivors—California—Los Angeles—Biography. Satu Mare
(Romania)—Biography. 6. Budapest (Hungary)—Biography. 7. Los Angeles
(Calif.)—Biography.   I. Title.
DS135.R73F37 1998
940.53'18'092—dc21
[B]   97-34615
                                                           CIP

For Ann, Danya, Jared, Andrew, and Kara

CONTENTS

Part One: Before the War

Ancsele (1931) 17
Szatmar 18
Games 19
Neighbors 22
Beggars 25
My Parents' Businesses 27
Perl 29
The Mikve 32
An Accident 33
A Bad Memory 35
First Grade and Glasses 37
Father Gets a New Job 39
Mamma's Business .41
Father Loses His Job 45
How Father Lost His Hearing 46
How Mamma Married Father 48
The Burdock Leaf 51
A Close Call 52
Neighbors, Gypsies, and a Dybbuk 54
A Death 57
The Holidays 58
Zishu 61
Szimu 62
Bucium 67
Secret Errands 73
Turc 73
Malku 80
Doctor Klein 82
Transylvania Is Returned to Hungary 84
Apprenticeship 86
We Are Going to America 92

Part Two: War Years

Fajgi and I Go to Budapest 97
Work and the Union 98
At Home for the Last Time, December 1943 105
Yellow Stars 112
Eva's Trip 113
Letters from Mamma 114
Laci Vamos 116
Rooster-Feathered Gendarmes 118
I Escape 124
Christian ID 130
Exempted Jews 130
Papers for Fajgi 133
Too Late to Save Fajgi 134
Swedish Passes and Wallenberg 135
I Buy Fajgi's Life 137
Death Marches 139
Margit and the Levais Go into Hiding 143
Eva Walks to Bergen-Belsen 145
On the Run 146
Arrow Cross Headquarters 154
Liberation 156
Russian Command Post 159
Home 161

Part Three: After the War

Struggling 175
Sanyi's Story 180
Remnants of Our Family 188
The Groza Train 190
Tibi 192
I Fall in Love 193
Mikola 194
Sanyi's Stories of Mikola 196

Married! 200
The House Where Sanyi Was Born 202
Early Years under Communism 211
Our Own Business 217
We Leave Romania 226
Los Angeles, California 228
Memories 240
Looking Back 241

Appendix

Rav Yoylish Teitelbaum: A Controversial Leader 245
Rezso Kasztner: Was He a Collaborator? 246
Raoul Wallenberg: Unsung Hero 247

Glossary 249
Bibliography 253

Acknowledgments

What follows would not have been written without my husband Alex and my daughter Ibi Winterman. Though I did not know Alex as a child, he grew up in the same town, a few blocks away from me, and he lived through the events I recount. He and I are as close to each other as it is possible for two different people to be. We talked over everything in this book. He served as a reality check for my facts, refreshed my memory by supplementing them with his own recollections, typed the first draft, drew the illustrations, and wrote most of Part Three.

Ibi insisted that I write my stories down, translated Part I from Hungarian, and edited Parts II and III. She went through the book word by word, paring down, explaining and rearranging. I had the final word on the contents of the book. But without the help of my husband and my daughter it would not have become a book.

I also want to thank my son-in-law Stanley Winterman, Don and Helene Weinstock, Drs. Harry Gonda and Clara Gonda, Dr. Louis Fridhandler, and Sara J. Mitchell.

Author's Note

In September 1944 I was walking on Nep Szinhaz Street in Budapest, taking a loaf of bread to my sister. As I was walking towards Teleki Square, I met a long procession of people surrounded by gendarmes. Grandparents, parents, and children were being driven down the middle of the street carrying infants and baggage, dragging children and suitcases after them. Some had a child in one arm, a suitcase in the other. On the sidewalk, people were going about their business, blind to the misery unfolding before their eyes. They were used to seeing Jews herded about and they couldn't care less. Then, an open truck filled with people just picked up from the streets approached from a side street. From the truck, someone shouted my name: "Rozsi, Rozsi, tell my parents they took me!" It was a friend, a girl named Margit. I felt people on the street turning to see whom she was calling. I looked around also, pretending she wasn't calling me. After all, I wasn't Rozsi Katz anymore. I was Ilona Kirtag.

Fifty years later, I can still hear her voice. That truck was taking her inexorably to the belly of a monster that devoured my mother, brothers, sisters, nieces, nephews, friends, and six million other Jews. A monster that I have eluded. Over the years I have been haunted by the question, "Why me? Why was I saved when so many others perished?"

I am not writing what follows to answer these questions. I am beginning to believe that there is no reason, no answer, that it is useless to try to understand. I am writing because there is in me a raging fear that soon it may be all forgotten. I cannot accept that when I die, the people who live in my memories may perish without a trace. Throughout my adult life, I have been reviewing in my mind the stories that follow. It was a way of keeping a vow not to forget those who have died. Now I feel that's not enough. I would like others to know all that I remember. If I could make them see in their mind's eye the house we lived in, the neighbors, the well where we went for drinking water, the place where my father worked, then perhaps that whole world won't become irretrievably lost.

~ *Part One* ~
BEFORE THE WAR

Ancsele *(1931)*

It was Friday evening after a hot summer day. I had already taken a bath and was wearing a clean, light green dress for *Shabbos*. I was playing outside with the other kids from our building. It wasn't dark yet. In our apartment, candles were burning in every room. We had electricity but on Fridays we didn't use it. Instead, before blessing the Shabbos candles, Mamma lighted candles in every room. On this night also, the candles were burning, filling the house with a festive spirit, but my younger brothers and I weren't allowed inside, where Mamma was struggling to bring her tenth child into the world. "Mrs. Stork," the midwife whose name wasn't really Mrs. Stork, had come to help her.

I was very important in the eyes of the neighbor children for being at the center of such an event. They had hundreds of questions for me and kept encouraging me to go inside and find out more definite details. We all believed that babies were brought by storks, and thought that Mrs. Stork had special connections with storks. We also knew that there were details being kept from us and were intent to find out more. I tried, but Mrs. Stork yelled at me, and shut the door in my face. I ran back to my friends. There was no question in our minds that Mrs. Stork was in charge at my house. There were sixteen other families in our building and it was the same Mrs. Stork who went to everybody's home when the stork brought a baby.

After what seemed like an eternity, I found out that I had another brother. Now I had three younger brothers: Szruel, who was four; Hershele, two; and the baby who was going to be called Ancsele. I also had a seventeen-year-old brother, Zishu, and five older sisters, Perl (nineteen), Szimu (fourteen), Hajcsu (twelve), Malku (ten), and Fajgi (nine). I, Ruchele Katz, was six years old. My parents were Ester and Aaron Katz. We all lived at 4 Kossuth Lajos Street, in Szatmar, Romania.

4 Kossuth Lajos Street

Szatmar

We lived in Romania but we all had Yiddish names, written with Hungarian spelling. At home we spoke Yiddish, and at school we were taught Romanian. But the majority of the population spoke only Hungarian, and we continued to use the old Hungarian names for the streets and the city.

Szatmar (Satu Mare in Romanian) has been a town for more than nine hundred years. It is situated in the north-western corner of Romania in a region called Erdely in Hungarian, Transylvania in Romanian. Transylvania had been part of the Austro-Hungarian Empire, but it was annexed to

Romania after the First World War. In the 1930s the town had a population of about 60,000, about one-third of whom were Jewish. Transylvania as a whole was home to a large number of Jewish people. They had come there encouraged by the enlightened policies of the Austro-Hungarian Empire.

There was little enmity between the Jews and non-Jews in Szatmar. They had been living side by side for generations. Most of the Jewish people were storekeepers, tradesmen, or artisans. Some held positions in Jewish community organizations. A few were prominent doctors or lawyers. Very few were rich. Some were middle-class. Most were poor or very poor. There were reform (also called status quo, statescu, or neologue) congregations and conservative congregations, but the overwhelming majority were strictly observant Orthodox or Chasidic Jews. My family was Orthodox and poor. Our lives were ruled by religious observance and oppressed by poverty.

Games

Our apartment house was a long one-story building with heavy double entry doors at its center. They led to a courtyard through a huge entrance hall. On both sides of the entrance hall, just past the entry doors, there were staircases of about eight steps leading up to a veranda onto which the apartments opened. On the window sills everybody had flower pots. My mamma had red geraniums in green wooden boxes. She also had flowers on a shelf on the veranda, under the kitchen window. In our building, we had the largest apartment. Most apartments had one or two bedrooms, but we had four since we occupied what were really two apartments.

High up in the entrance hall, in front of the staircases to the veranda, were two pairs of windows. The ones on the left belonged to us. The two on the right belonged to Mrs. Eisner, a widow, whose children were all grown. The large entrance hall echoed with children's voices.

It was our favorite place to play and the only place to play ball because in the yard every family had a little garden under its apartment. Annoyed with the noise we made, Mrs. Eisner would open her window and throw a bucket of cold water on us. We didn't like getting wet and would keep away for a while. Pretty soon we drifted back to the entrance hall. We learned to accept cold water striking down at us from above as part of the order of things. Mrs. Eisner must have learned to carry in extra buckets of water for that purpose, since there was no running water in the apartments. The entrance hall was also a good place for playing hide-and-seek since two stairways to the cellar under the building started from there. I was always scared when I hid in the cellar because I believed that ghosts lurked in the shadows. The other kids were even more afraid than I, so nobody could find me when I hid there.

It was also fun to jump down from the veranda to the ground, though we couldn't do it for long because this also bothered Mrs. Eisner. The other place to play was the sidewalk, in front of the house. We played hopscotch there but that meant running into trouble with the caretaker who didn't like the chalk markings on the concrete.

Along the sidewalk there were some old acacia trees. In the spring they were covered with clusters of white flowers which had a heavenly fragrance and tasted like honey, if you knew how to extract the nectar from them. In the summer we congregated in the shade of the trees to watch the ice cream vendor. The sweat was dripping down his face from pushing his two-wheeled cart. He always stopped in front of our house and rang his bell. With so many children living in the building, he knew that he could count on some who would be successful in wrangling some change from their

Entrance hall

parents. The lucky customers stood on the cart's wheel and pointed inside the cart at the flavor they wanted. The rest of us watched respectfully while the vendor filled the cones.

Also on the street, on both sides of the entry doors, there were two stores with a few steps and a small landing. The steps were flanked with low, shiny concrete sides instead of banisters. Those walls were good to slide down on, but that too got us into trouble. I could never understand why so many grownups would get so angry so often. We were just children trying to have a little fun. We were pretty ingenious when it came to entertaining ourselves.

One summer evening, some older boys from our building set some paper money on the side walk, tied a thread to it, and hid behind the doors, holding on to the thread. It was almost dusk, so you couldn't see the thread. We were all watching through the cracks of the entry doors. A passerby came along, saw the money and tried to pick it up. The boys pulled on the string. The man kept reaching for the money and the boys kept pulling on the string, until the money disappeared and we all burst into thunderous laughter. Then the man knew he was being made a fool of and went away sheepishly. It was capital fun and it worked with quite a few passersby.

After a while, a boy from a few houses down walked by. He must have known the trick because he did not reach for the money. Instead he stepped on it, then bent down, grabbed it and ran away. Our boys ran after him and it all ended in a tremendous free-for-all. But by then it was completely dark and time to go inside.

Neighbors

The most beloved (respected and well-to-do) family in our building was the Zusmans. Mrs. Zusman talked things over with Mamma but she didn't associate with any of the other neighbors. I was aware of the social implications of her accepting Mamma as her one equal and basked in the reflected glory. Mr. Zusman was a tall, handsome man with a well-groomed beard. I knew he was rich because he wore Shabbos clothes even on weekdays.

He owned a pub on the little market street. Sometimes, on hot summer days, Mamma sent me there for a glass of beer. I had to run home very fast because she liked to have a little foam left on top. All the way home I checked if the foam was still there.

The pub was always full of people. On Wednesdays the customers were mostly peasants who came to sell their produce at the weekly market.

They drank if they sold their merchandise and they drank if they didn't, though maybe not quite as much. Mr. Zusman had a good business.

On Saturdays, the Zusmans' daughter Surika wore a beautiful navy blue velvet dress with a white lace collar. I liked that dress very much and wanted one just like it. They also had a son, Hilu, who wore a satin coat that came to his knees and long, twisted *peyes* (ear locks). He was so religious he would not walk between two girls. He kept interrupting our playing with his coming and going. He would stand by the wall and ask us to stand on one side so he could pass. It didn't make him very popular with us girls.

Mr. Zusman had a good business

The Zusmans also had two grown children, a daughter, Etu, who would come to visit with her children, and another son, Chaim, who was Mr. Zusman's son from an earlier marriage. Chaim, tall and very handsome, came rarely and never stayed long. After he left, Mrs. Zusman would always complain to Mamma about how *ausgelassent* he was, how he didn't keep any of the religious customs. She didn't like her stepson and she always complained about him. I listened to her in wonder. We were always worried about doing things in accordance with religious custom and I knew that even small deviations could have grave consequences. I couldn't understand why God didn't punish Chaim.

We rented the room between our apartment and the Zusmans' to the Adlers. They had no children but they kept pigeons in a cage high on a column of the veranda. I liked to watch how devoted the pigeons were to each other and to listen to their cooing. They reminded me of Mr. and Mrs. Adler. Mr. Adler was a shoemaker. He was a small man, always neatly dressed. He didn't have a beard, and that meant he was "modern." Their tiny, one-room apartment served for bedroom, kitchen, and shop. They had one hutch in which his tools and boot trees were stored and another hutch that held cups and plates and a magnificent set of pots and pans, red on the outside and white on the inside. They also had two beds, a table, and two chairs. It was always incredibly neat and clean there, and they always had room for visiting children.

Mr. Adler told us stories

I used to watch Mr. Adler work for hours, sitting next to him on a three-legged stool. A green apron spread on his knees to protect his clothing, he made a hole in the sole of a shoe with an awl and then he quickly filled it with a wooden nail. He knew how to make new shoes but most of his work was fixing old ones. He told us stories while he worked. I liked to visit there. There was always a smile on his face when he saw me, a smile framed by a beautiful mustache.

Then tragedy struck. Mrs. Adler started to go crazy. She got worse and worse, and soon we were too afraid to visit. One day some men in uniform put her in a straitjacket and took her to the asylum in Sziget. We heard that she died a short time later. Little Mr. Adler sold what he could, packed up the rest of his things, and went back to Poland. I lost a true friend and my family regained a room.

Beggars

With the room that used to belong to the Adlers we had a five-room apartment. But we were still so crowded that we slept *tsu fis un tsu kopens*, two to a bed, head to feet. I always woke up in a bed different from the one I went to sleep in. Mamma got up before dark every morning.

Sometimes, wakened by the light and edged on by my curiosity, I got up too to see what she was doing. She sat next to the kitchen door on a small bench, holding a prayer book. She was praying Thilem. She did this every morning when the whole house was still asleep. As a truly pious woman, Mamma did everything to make sure that her children grew up religiously observant. The boys went to *cheder* every week day.

The girls were taught to read and write Hebrew by a teacher who came to the house. It was serious business. We had to stop playing, find our notebooks and pencils, and get down to work the moment he arrived.

Hebrew lessons

Mamma also observed the commandment to give
tzedaka. From early morning on Thursday till noon on Friday, a procession of *schnorrers* (professional beggars) came to
our house. Even though our own livelihood was precarious,
our door was always open to them. On Wednesday night we
threaded half leu pieces, which had a hole in the middle,
making long strings of coins for the beggars. I remember
that Mrs. Zusman, whose door was always closed to beggars,
was outraged. *"Frau Katz, Zi haben gegeben tsu dis schnorrer*
[You have given to that beggar]! He is a rich man. He owns
his own house in Sziget and he has the nerve to beg from
you!" But Mamma always said, "If you are asked, you have to
give." I thought Mrs. Zusman was right, and wished
Mamma would listen to her. We could have used that money
ourselves. Besides, Mrs. Zusman, the richest and most re-

spected person in the building, didn't give money to schnorrers. She kept her doors shut while our doors were always open. It seemed to me that God should make Mamma listen to Mrs. Zusman, and that He should make Mrs. Zusman give tzedaka instead of us.

My Parents' Businesses

I often wondered why we were so poor when Mamma's family, the Benovitses, were rich. When I got older I learned that Mamma's family had tried to help us several times. My parents were unlucky when it came to business. Father had used Mamma's dowry to buy a lumber mill at Karan Sebes. They manufactured planks and construction lumber. They employed many lumberjacks and did quite well for a while. Then the First World War came, and Father was drafted. The demand for building materials declined and, with two little ones and a third one on the way, Mamma could not take care of what business was left. By the time the war was finished the mill was also finished.

After the war, my family moved to Szatmar and my parents started over. The Benovitses gave them a large sum of money which Mamma and Father used to open a salt warehouse. Again for a while they prospered, even exporting salt. Then the Szamos River overflowed and their warehouse, which was in a cellar, flooded. The water melted the salt and washed it away. That was the end of that business.

Next Mamma's parents helped them open a grocery store in the building we lived in. It was a room which opened onto the street but was connected to the rest of our apartment. We sold mostly on credit. For each family there was a small book with numbers, showing how much was owed. People paid us when they could and my parents made a modest living.

Then, in the building next door to ours, the Schreibers

opened another grocery store. We lived at 4 Kossuth Lajos Street, the Schreibers at number 2. The neighborhood couldn't possibly support two stores and the Depression had made it difficult for people to pay their bills. With a new store offering fresh credit, our customers deserted us. We were left with lots of little books full of numbers and no money to pay our bills or buy new merchandise. That was the end of our grocery store.

Our grocery store

After that, Mamma wouldn't accept any more money from her parents. Father got a job at the big slaughterhouse by the river, and Mamma converted our grocery store into a bedroom for us, and rented out another bedroom that had a separate entry from the veranda to Mr. and Mrs. Adler. She also started a business of her own, buying geese and selling the meat and by-products. Her family still helped us. Each summer when Mamma went to visit her parents in Csaszloc,

Czechoslovakia, she came back loaded down with clothes for the children and things for the house. We also got packages from Mamma's brother in America and Mamma was willing to ask for help for exceptional expenses. But our day-to-day life was a struggle to make ends meet. Mamma was always full of financial worries.

Perl

Ancsele was born in 1931, when I was six years old. But I remember things that happened earlier. My oldest memory is being hard at play outside when my sister Fajgi called me in. Mamma wanted us to take lunch to Perl, my oldest sister. I ran into the house, washed my face and hands, and was ready to take on the world. But first I took a detour to our grocery store to provision myself with some sugar cubes for the road. I had to climb a ladder to reach the sugar drawer. Under me, there was a wall of drawers containing rice, beans, and all sorts of groceries. On the very bottom, instead of drawers, there were large built-in bins with different grades of flour.

I put the sugar cubes in my pocket and Fajgi and I started out. We walked down Eotvos Street, cut across the park at the center of the town, and arrived at the Ostereicher House, where Perl was working.

In the workshop, girls were sitting in long lines weaving Persian rugs. Perl's fingers moved faster than a machine. Her rug was so beautiful that even the other girls working there came to look at it. Perl herself was a beautiful girl. I was proud of being her sister. Mamma was proud of her, too. She was always telling our neighbor, Mrs. Zusman, what good money Perl brought home, how small were the knots she could tie, and how much faster she was than any of the other girls.

When Perl was eighteen, a marriage broker came to offer a *shidech* for her. The young man's name was Avrum Gluck.

I climbed the ladder

He was nineteen, tall and handsome, and had no practical education or occupation. The important thing was that he had been a Talmud student and was a religious *bocher*. Mamma wrote to her oldest brother, Moric Benovits, who lived in America with his wife, Aunt Zsenka, and their only daughter, Alice. She asked him to send a dowry for Perl. She was asking for fifty thousand lei, the going rate for a dowry among people like us, and more money than my father earned in two years. There could be no wedding until the money was paid to the groom. Uncle Moric, who had a re-frigerator factory, was rich and he was a good brother. Soon there came an announcement from the bank that the money had arrived, and a wedding date was set. Mamma had a long, thick, gold chain that had been part of her own dowry. She cut off a part of it and sold it to pay for the wedding.

At Mamma's suggestion, and at her expense of course, Avrum learned the craft of being a *shoychet,* a ritual slaughterer. Mamma even bought the special knives he needed. It was a good craft and in a short time Avrum obtained a position in a little village named Bucium, near Somkut. There were at most twenty Jewish families in Bucium, so it wasn't well paid. But the position included housing, and it was secure. A shoychet was a necessity for every Jewish community. Mamma was happy. In those days it was difficult for a poor girl to get married and Perl's destiny had been settled in a satisfactory manner. Mamma still had five more girls to marry off, but a heavy load had been lifted from her heart.

A year later, in 1931, Perl and Avrum had their first child, a son. Mamma was expecting her tenth child at the same as Perl was expecting her first. Perl's baby arrived at the same time as a notice that Avrum was to be drafted into the army. This was a tremendous setback. It meant that he would be separated from his family and unable to support them for three years. He had been lucky to get a job in the first place, and now he was sure to lose it. Worst of all, he would be unable to observe Jewish dietary laws and religious customs for years. Crying in despair, Mrs. Gluck, the *makheteyneste,* who was even poorer than we were, came to Mamma for help. Mamma sold another piece of her necklace and arranged for Avrum to become a *Schimbash,* a volunteer artillery cadet. It was a racket, involving army officers and suppliers. Avrum had to provide his own food, uniform, and horse and saddle, but instead of three years, he only had to serve three months.

Mamma had paid money to the horse dealer who supplied the horse, the saddle maker who supplied the regulation saddle, the veterinarian who certified that the horse was healthy, the person who knew the sergeant Avrum was to serve under, the sergeant himself, the colonel, and the people filling every rank in between. But Avrum was saved.

The Mikve

I didn't think Perl's getting married was worth all the fuss everyone was making. I liked it better when she lived at home with us. But there was one good thing about it. Mrs. Gluck, Perl's mother-in-law, worked at the *mikve*, the public bath house. Since most families didn't have bathrooms, the bath house was an important institution. It was a long, low building on Vardomb Street. Inside the main entrance, tickets were sold at the window of a small office. A stairway with copper railings and about six steps led down to a long, narrow hallway. A wooden lattice covered the wet, tiled floor. The long hallway was dotted on both sides with doors through which filtered the sounds of children laughing and playing happily in the bath water. Between the doors, benches lined the walls for those waiting to get in.

Mamma gathered us up to go to the mikve once a week. After Perl's wedding, Mrs. Gluck always gave us special treatment. She greeted us with obvious pleasure and gossiped with Mamma a few minutes. She didn't have much time to talk because as soon as one family left, it was her job to wash out the bath tub and get the room ready for the next customers. There were other women who worked there but Mrs. Gluck always insisted on taking care of us personally. She told us that she wanted to make sure that our tub was clean, and she would even wash it twice for us just to be sure. I felt we were treated like royalty and loved it.

Each bathing room was about twelve feet by ten. The

floor, tub, and walls were covered with white tiles. There were hooks on the wall and benches for changing. A sunken tub took up half the room. It could have easily held ten people, but usually it was just Mamma, my younger brothers, and I. Because we were her honored guests, Mrs. Gluck came in and added more hot water for us. If anybody had found out, we would have had to pay double, so it had to be done secretly. And the secrecy made the bath even more luxurious and special. We sat and played in the tub till we were all pink from the heat and glowing with cleanliness.

An Accident

I have treasured memories of visits to Mamma's cousin Aunt Etelka. Aunt Etelka and her family lived in the suburb Major. They ran a general store in a house that once contained the famous Szatmari Csarda Inn, which is mentioned in a poem by Sandor Petoefi.

They had a huge, grassy garden with large trees beyond which there was nothing but open fields. I went there with my older sisters to play with our cousins. We loved to go there and often spent the whole day with them.

We took the levee bordering Homorod Brook past the bridge across the Szamos River early in the morning and returned in the late afternoon on Hegyi Road. The levee's sides were covered with soft, green grass and I used to run and tumble up and down on them. In the summer, the Homorod was harmless. In early spring, swollen with runoff from the melting snow, it rose to the top of the levee, and at the railroad bridge, where the Homorod met the Szamos River, the waters whirled and foamed like an inferno. In some years, when the danger from flooding was imminent, the levee on the other side of Homorod was cut and the fields outside the city were submerged.

In the summer it was shallow and slow. I would take off

my shoes and run splashing in the lukewarm water, trying to catch dragonflies among the willow trees. I saw the cows and horses feeding in the pastures lining the levee on the other side of the brook. Sometimes I met a little boy or girl leading a lamb or goat by a rope. Just to go to Aunt Etelka's house was an adventure.

Once on the way home, busy talking with each other, my sisters fell behind. I was far ahead of them, almost at the bridge, when suddenly a bicyclist rang his bell behind me. I tried to get out of his way but when I went right, he went right, and when I went left he went left. In the end, he ran me down. Frightened, my sisters ran to me and picked me

They tried to wash the blood off

up. Blood was pouring from my face.

They carried me across the bridge to the well in front of Mr. Kato's bakery to wash the blood off. They couldn't stop the bleeding so they took me to Mr. Tabaydi's pharmacy, which was on the corner across from the bakery. Mr. Tabaydi knew me because he was also our landlord. He cleaned and dressed my wound and he told me, "Little Katz girl, you'll forget all about it by the time you get married." He was wrong. There weren't enough tranquil, sunshine-filled years left for the memory to fade.

My sisters bought me a bag of candy from Elefants' grocery store, which was next door to the bakery. They told me to go straight to bed when we got home without saying anything to Mamma. I did as they asked me but Mamma wasn't used to my being quiet or uninterested in dinner. When she came to check on me and saw the bandage near my eye, the whole story came out. She scolded my sisters for not taking better care of me and thanked God that I didn't lose an eye. I was pleased that she was so concerned. I still have a little hollow depression next to my left eye—and I hear Mamma's concerned voice every time I see it in the mirror.

A Bad Memory

I have a bad memory from about that time. Across the street from us, at 1 Kossuth Lajos Street, stood the Statescu Temple. It took up the whole width of the block on Eotvos Street, and half a block each of Eminescu Street and Kossuth Lajos Street. It was a beautiful, red brick building surrounded by a hand-crafted wrought iron fence and evergreen bushes that poked through the fence. Walkways covered with white pebbles and bordered by a low boxwood hedge led up to the main entrance and the side doors.

Beyond the hedge were beds of perennials and flowering shrubs, and beyond the flower beds were well-kept green lawns with huge wild chestnut trees. It was a land of marvels and wonders that increased as you approached the building. It had huge oak entry doors, carved with flowers and palm branches, and tall, narrow windows with stained-glass inserts. Inside, the blue ceiling painted with gold stars was supported by carved columns. The red velvet drapes in front of the ark were embroidered with gold. (The building no longer exists. It survived the war but, under the communist regime, the city authorities dismantled it to use the brick for other purposes. In its place they built a box building housing the offices of the local state security agency and the police and detention facilities.)

The Statescu Temple

Many people belonged to that congregation, but we didn't. We were much more religious than the people who went there. We were so religious that, on Saturdays, my parents even tied their handkerchiefs around their necks if they went anywhere. That's because by tying the handkerchief around one's neck, one was wearing it, not carrying it. As Orthodox Jews my parents could not carry anything outside their house on Shabbos in a town like Szatmar, which did not have an *eirev*, or wall, around it. Had there been a wall around our city, it would have been okay to carry things because then it would have been possible to regard the whole town as the inside of a house. Such complex reasoning seemed self-evident to me at age five.

Strictures about carrying didn't apply to small children who were too young to observe them. One Shabbos, I was playing outside on the street in the front of our store when, from the other side of the street, a man with his prayer shawl in one hand and a bag of candies in the other hand called me over. He wanted me to carry his *talles,* his prayer shawl, to the Statescu Temple in exchange for the bag of candy. Of course I agreed. I didn't notice that no one was at the temple, and it didn't occur to me that since he was going to the re-form temple he could have carried his own talles. I was too busy anticipating the candy. He told me that I should hold the talles very tight because God would punish me if I dropped it. I thought, "He doesn't need to tell me that." I had known it for a long time. We reached the Temple but, to my surprise, he passed the entrance to the Temple and went to the staircase door of the Temple office. Behind the door, he gave me the candy but instead of taking the talles from me he picked me up and started to fondle me and tear at me roughly in places that I knew he wasn't supposed to touch. I didn't know what to do. He was hurting me. But if I ran away, I would be stealing his talles. If I threw down the talles and ran, God would punish me for dropping it. If I stayed, I was sure to die of what he was doing to me. I was in an im-possible situation, so I thought I might as well do what I most felt like. I kicked him, threw down the talles and the candy, and ran. The whole time I was waiting for God to strike me down for the way I had handled the talles, but He didn't. So I began to doubt that God sees everything.

First Grade and Glasses

I loved school passionately. It was a totally new and different world. I befriended new kids, I met people who were not Jewish, and I learned Romanian (at home we spoke Hungarian and Yiddish). We had a wonderful teacher, Domnisoara Anica. She lived at the end of Arpad Street in a house with a big garden. A few of us walked her home every day after school.

We hung on her, wanting to hold her hand, or if we couldn't be that close to her, we wanted just to be near her. I could hardly wait for morning so I could see her again. I was seriously in love and to please her I made sure I got all A's on my report card.

A few of us walked her home

Some of the children in my class wore glasses. I admired their glasses and I decided that I wanted a pair also. I told Mamma that I couldn't see well. She took me to the optometrist, Dr. Samu Fekete. He asked me to read the smallest letters on the eye chart that I could see. Wanting to make sure that I would get glasses, I told him I could only read the top line. He told Mamma that I was seriously near-sighted and he prescribed glasses for me. I could hardly wait for them to be made. When I finally got them and put them on, I saw big holes in front of me and I was afraid to take a step. I had glasses but couldn't wear them. Mamma kept nagging me to put on my glasses. I didn't dare tell her the truth.

The only other time I went to a doctor was when I had a tooth-ache. Mamma sent me to the Catholic Priests' Hospital because they didn't charge for extracting a tooth. The hospital was quite far from our house. I had to walk down Eotvos Street, cross the big park in the city square, and continue on Kazincy Street past the convent to Hospital Street. As I passed the convent I met a row of nuns in long black robes and crisp white bonnets, walking in pairs. I wondered who they had been before they became nuns. There was a small park on Hospital Street. In the back of the park were the Commercial School, the big City Hospital, and at the far end, the smaller white building of the Priests' Hospital.

Big black crosses on the walls of the waiting room and the hallways made me feel uncomfortable. When it was my turn, I entered the office, sat in the chair, and showed the dentist which tooth hurt, while trying not to look at his tools. He was done in no time.

On the way home I had to pass by the Commercial School. A penetrating stink of cabbage emanated from the huge cellar windows where the kitchen was located. I felt sorry for those who had to eat there.

Father Gets a New Job

In 1933, a new slaughterhouse for poultry was built on Vardomb Street, next to the big *shul* (temple). Mamma had a second cousin, Aunt Tila, whose husband, Mr. Davidovics, was the executive director of the orthodox congregation. Mamma asked Aunt Tila to get a job for Father at the new slaughterhouse. He had been working at the slaughterhouse on the bank of the Szamos River, where only big animals were slaughtered, and the work was becoming too hard for him. It was also far from home and poorly paid. I remember how happy Mamma was when she told us that Aunt Tila had promised that Father would get a position at the new slaughterhouse.

Aunt Tila kept her word. In his new post, Father sold tickets in exchange for which poultry was slaughtered. People queued up in front of the window of his tiny office to buy the *gabela* ticket. After that they stood in line between iron rails skirting a long rectangular basin that crossed the middle of the room. The basin had built-in sprinklers on the sides and hooks on a low wall along the middle. The queue led them to two large windows overlooking the basin. Behind the windows, two shoychets worked in a separate room. People handed over their bird, legs tied together, and their ticket through the windows. The shoychet handed back the slaughtered bird that was then hung from one of the hooks above the basin till the blood ran out. The basin had built-in sprinklers to rinse away the blood. It was very efficient.

In addition, a free enterprise zone flourished. To determine if a duck or goose was kosher, the vayshet (crop) had to be inspected by the *dayan* (judge) whose office was at the other end of the room near the exit. If the dayan found the duck or goose to be kosher, the *mashgiach* (supervisor of ritual correctness), Mr. Ancsel, who happened to be related to the dayan, stamped the kosher seal on the bird. Someone had to extract the crop and some people didn't know how or didn't want to do this for themselves. So in the back, along the width of the room, tables were set up where women working for themselves could be hired to extract the crop. They could also be hired to pull out the feathers of a chicken for a leu or two. Duck and goose feathers were valuable, so people did not have ducks or geese cleaned at the slaughterhouse.

Mamma's Business

In third grade I started skipping school every Wednesday to help Mamma with making our *parnusi,* our family's livelihood. We went to the weekly poultry market on Bathanyi Street to buy fat geese. We left at dawn because that was when one could get the best buys. When Mamma bought a goose I watched it while she went to buy another one. Then she bought another one and another one still, and I had to watch them all.

The poultry market

When her money was all gone and we had ten or twelve geese, the peasant who sold her the last goose gave us and our geese a ride home in his wagon. Mamma had included the ride in the bargain. The whole way home, we sat on the wagon watching that, *cholile,* God forbid, a goose didn't suffocate or fall out and die.

Mamma sold the meat, fat, *griveleh* (roasted skin), and

liver of the geese. If we were lucky, a big liver paid for the whole goose. I took the big livers to Helena Klein, who had an exporting business. A small liver wasn't so valuable and we sold it to one of our own customers.

By the time we got home with the geese it was pretty late in the day. We put the geese into one of the wooden sheds that lined the backyard, one for each apartment. I ran to bring them a dish of fresh water, and I untied their feet and wings. Then Mamma and I went to the little market on Eotvos Street to buy vegetables and fruit.

We never bought milk or dairy products at the market. Those were delivered to our home by an old Jewish man who had a wagon drawn by a blind horse. I wondered how the horse was able to find its way to so many different places.

There were eight rows of tents and tables. If the peasants brought in a lot of same kind of fruit, it was cheap. If only a few of them brought the same kind of fruit, it was expensive. I learned the law of supply and demand. Since fruit was expensive and we needed so much of everything, we often went back to the market just before it closed. That's when you could buy left-over fruit very inexpensively because the peasants didn't want to carry it back home with them.

Sometimes I ran home with the full baskets and ran back with empty ones to buy even more. Often the basket handles wore deep red marks into my hands and my arms ached so much that I thought they'd break. But I never complained. I loved being able to help Mamma.

Mamma ran her goose business with money she borrowed from Itzhak Rosenberg, a feed merchant who lived in a big house that he owned at 8 Kossuth Lajos Street, two houses away from us. We borrowed money on Tuesday nights and paid it back on Fridays after selling the meat. Apparently there was never enough left for capital, for we went on borrowing from them week after week. The Rosenbergs were also customers, and I often took them meat, liver and

The fruit market

griveleh for Shabbos.

They had four sons who were grown men when I was still a child. Shulem, Shmilu, and Laibi were good-looking and tall. They wore Shabbos clothes every day. Once when I was there during a weekday lunch I saw that their table was set for Shabbos even on weekdays. They had beautiful plates and serving dishes, shiny silverware, and a lot of wonderfully fragrant food.

The fourth son, Nuszi, was bedridden and for months I helped take care of him for a couple of hours a day. His skin had a yellow pallor and he had so little strength he couldn't get out of bed. If he needed a chamber pot I put it under him. After that I pulled it out and emptied it in the bathroom. When he wanted water, I gave it to him gladly. As a nine year old, I was very proud to be able to nurse a big man like him. I asked Mamma whether he would die because he was getting worse every day. She said that some germs were eating him from inside and that he was dying. Soon afterwards he did die. I felt very sorry for him and his family.

On Wednesday nights, by the time I came home from the Rosenbergs, the geese and poultry were ready to be taken to the shoychet's house to be slaughtered. We all helped carry them over. After we got back, we all helped pull out the feathers till late into the night.

Thursday at dawn, Mamma cut open the geese. She laid each bird on its stomach and made a vertical cut down its back with a sharp knife. Near the leg, she had to cut diagonally across. She had to be really careful at this point so as not to damage the precious liver. Cutting open a goose was always accompanied by a lot of excitement. With each goose we prayed that it would have a big liver. (I wondered about that, too. Didn't the goose already have the liver it had? Could praying make a difference?)

Even more important, we prayed that each goose would be kosher. If, God forbid, the dayan saw anything wrong with its *vayshet* (crop), the goose would become *treyfe* (not kosher) and we would have to sell it at a great loss to a non-Jew. We would extract the crops and Father would run over to the dayan with them. I can still hear him call from afar, on his way back home: *"Ester, di gendzen zenen ale kosher* [Ester, the geese are all kosher]." Father didn't know Hungarian. He and Mamma spoke Yiddish to each other or, when they wanted to keep something from us children, Czech.

By the time Father returned with the news, the livers were extracted. If there were three big livers we were lucky. I remember how excited Mamma was on those occasions. She weighed the big livers on the scale and Father figured out how much we would be paid for them. I was dispatched immediately to take the livers over to Helena Klein's. They always weighed less on Helena Klein's scale than they did on Mamma's scale. This made me very angry and I argued with her and her husband. I told them that God would punish them if they were cheating us. They would laugh and tell me that the liver dried up between the time it sat on Mamma's scale and the time it was put on their scale. I knew that wasn't true but they were the only buyers in town and if they said it weighed less, we had to accept it. I hated being cheated, and didn't like having to wait for God to punish them, but there was nothing I could do but fume.

Father Loses His Job

We would take the geese to the home of one of the shoychets, late at night on Wednesdays. At home, he charged only half price to slaughter the geese. Not having to buy the gabela tickets was a little extra profit and having the geese slaughtered on Wednesdays gave us time to get the meat ready for Thursday morning customers.

This went on for a long time. The shoychet, who had eight children and couldn't make ends meet from his salary alone, slaughtered geese at home for other people also. Then someone denounced him to the Community Council for working at home. To our misfortune, when the representatives of the Community Council came to his house to investigate the matter, Father was found there with our slaughtered geese. Since Father was also working at the slaughterhouse, it looked bad. Father and the shoychet were accused of conspiring to defraud the Community Council. They were both locked up in separate rooms in the Victoria Hotel, which was owned by Elmer Weisz, until the Council established the facts and decided what should be done about them. There was talk of firing both my father and the shoychet. If Father lost his job, it would have been very difficult for him to find another, equally good job. Father was deaf. In this job people just showed him the poultry and he didn't have to hear. So losing his job would have been a great tragedy for us.

Finally, after a few days, the Council decided to remove Father from his original position and made him the mashgiach, the supervisor of ritual correctness and caretaker of the slaughter house. This was due in large part to Mamma's behind-the-scene maneuverings through the help of her cousin Tila Davidovics. But it wasn't a good solution. The place already had a mashgiach—Mr. Ancsel, who was related to the dayan. There was no need for two mashgiachs, but they could neither dismiss Mr. Ancsel, who also had a lot of small children, nor find him another job right away. So for a while there were two mashgiachs and they spent the day eyeing each other angrily.

Though Father still had a job, his new assignment was less prestigious and paid less money. As time passed Father became sadder and more discouraged. I rarely saw him smile.

How Father Lost His Hearing

Mamma told me the story of how father lost his hearing. It happened in the First World War. The war started in 1914, when Archduke Ferdinand of Austria was assassinated in Sarajevo. My father was drafted even though he had two small children and Mamma was pregnant with a third. It was a terrible war. People died by the tens of thousands on the battlefields.

Once, during the war, Father came home on leave. Because the war strained transportation resources, soldiers were traveling in cattle wagons furnished with benches that were not nailed down. Father had fallen asleep on a bench and when the soldier who was sitting on the other end of the bench got up, he fell down. Father thought the soldier made him fall intentionally and, enraged, got into a fist fight with him. They were separated by the other passengers but they stayed angry with each other.

Then something funny happened. Father had to take another train to get to Szatmar. When it was time to transfer, the soldier he had fought with transferred to the same train. When Father got off the train at Szatmar, the stranger got off also. When Father left the station, the stranger left in the same direction. When Father turned onto our street, the stranger followed. Father started to climb the stairs to our apartment, and the stranger was still behind him. And then, Mamma saw them through our door, which was always open, and she ran to them and hugged them both. The stranger was Feter Hershel, the husband of her younger sister, Elke, whom Father had never met. Feter Hershel had been on his way home to Batyu and he had decided to stop on the way to visit us.

Not much later Mamma received notice that Father died at the front. A mountainside collapsed because of shelling, and Father and his whole unit were buried under it. Saint Bernard dogs were used to find the bodies, which were dug out and piled up in pits filled with lime until they could be properly buried. The sanitation officer responsible for burying the bodies happened to be Feter Hershel. Because of the earlier incident, he recognized Father and pulled him out from among the bodies piled in the pit. It turned out Father still had a little life left in him and Feter Hershel revived him. And that's how Father stayed alive. But he had lost most of his hearing when the mountain collapsed on him. One had to shout loudly for him to hear.

His deafness isolated Father from his children. He could read Mamma's lips when she spoke Yiddish but we spoke Hungarian and he was unable to learn it since we moved to Hungarian-speaking Szatmar after he became deaf. In addition, he was rarely home, and when he was at home, it was his job to discipline us. For some reason, he had a special relationship with Hershele, who always sat on his lap during Friday night dinners and Saturday lunches. From the rest of us, he settled for respect.

How Mamma Married Father

I worshipped Mamma and didn't have much use for Father. I wondered how Mamma could have married him. There was a story behind that also.

Mamma's parents, the Benovitses, were rich farmers in Csaszloc, Czechoslovakia. They had cattle and large fields to graze them on. Father's parents were neither as rich nor as well educated. They lived in Hukliva, a small, isolated village in the Carpathian Mountains, where they owned a forest. Father was the oldest of five sons. His father and his brothers worked from dawn till dusk harvesting trees for the lumber mills. Father, who worked alongside them since his childhood, had a harsh life.

Harvesting trees for lumber mills

Father was strong and handsome, so when a sidech was proposed, Mamma's parents accepted it. But after thinking about it, they decided that the social difference between Mamma and Father was too great and they canceled the engagement. A short time later, a terrible cattle epidemic decimated the Benovitses' herds. Their Rabbi decided that it was punishment for having humiliated Father and his family and that it wouldn't stop until they offered reparation. So Mamma's parents sent for Father and the wedding was held. Still with serious second thoughts about the match, they had resigned themselves to the marriage only provisionally, as it were. They thought that, after a little while, Mamma could obtain a *get,* a divorce, and follow her brother Moric to America. In those days even thinking about a divorce was unheard of so Mamma's parents must have been very unhappy about the marriage. But once married to Father, Mamma decided she didn't want to divorce him.

It is only now that I realize that as a child I was unfair to Father. He was strict and exacting at home and his deafness made him suspicious and liable to misinterpret our actions. But he also worshipped Mamma and he was devoted to his family. He worked as hard as he could to support us at poorly paid jobs. Although he worked very hard at his jobs outside the house, he helped Mamma with everything. He was always working. He and Mamma never argued. They never even raised their voices to each other. He also tried to make sure that we grew into good people and observant Jews at a time when the world conspired against Jews with both secular enticements and savage discrimination. He did the best he could with the hand he was dealt.

After Father's demotion, I decided I wanted to help more. On my visits to Father's work, I had watched the women take out the crops of the ducks and geese and clean the chickens and I knew I could do that, too. And I knew that on Thursdays, the slaughterhouse was so busy there would be work for me. So I stayed out from school on Thursdays as well as Wednesdays. My teacher, Miss Anica, understood. Stroking my face she told me that I was a good girl.

I went to work armed with two big nails and a pillowcase. I needed a nail to open up the skin of the geese to get at the crop. The other women used their thumbs but my hands were not strong enough for that. I took two nails in case one got lost. Goose feathers were not plucked at the slaughterhouse because they were valuable. But to get at the crop the skin had to be bared at the neck. I gathered the handful of feathers I plucked from each goose and put them in the pillowcase.

With a nail, I broke the skin on the left side of the neck, reached in deep with my fingers and pulled out the crop, wrapping it on my finger to get it all out. Then I cleaned the crop and blew it up like a balloon, twisting the two ends so that the air wouldn't escape. If I saw that the crop was translucent I would tell the owner in advance that the goose was going to be judged kosher. The owner would smile and say, "*Vosser a meyvn* [what a specialist]!" Sometimes I lost both nails in the pillowcase of feathers, and there wasn't time to look for them. Everybody was in a hurry. Then, I would break open the skin by biting into it. I remember getting curious, respectful glances for my grit and determination.

I got one leu for each crop. The first day was over before I noticed. I was working with such fervor, I even forgot to eat. At the end of the day, I had made thirty-nine lei, and I had a little pillowcase of goose feathers. It was my first pay and more money than I had ever held in my hands before. From then on I went to work at the slaughterhouse every Thursday. It was hard work and my hands hurt by the end of the day but I was happy and proud to be able to help Mamma.

At the slaughterhouse, at lunch time, an old man used to come in and sell cheese Danish from a big, flat basket, but I couldn't bear to spend the money on it. One day, when I made a little more money than usual, I bought a Danish for two lei. It smelled so delicious and I had wanted it for such a long time, I simply could not resist the desire any longer. When I bit into it, I felt I was in heaven. I'll never forget its taste. With that one exception, I always gave all my earnings to Mamma.

The Burdock Leaf

Once Mamma cut her middle finger on a bone while cutting open a goose. She bandaged it and went on with her work. After a few days her whole hand turned blue and she developed a very high fever. We were all frightened that she was about to die. We took her to the hospital where she was given some medicine that made her sleep. In her sleep she dreamt that her dead grandmother brought her a burdock leaf and tied it to her finger. When she woke up, the leaf was there on her finger and she was feeling better. When Mamma told us that story, I was sure that God put that leaf on her finger because He didn't want her to die yet. Mamma's middle finger was permanently bent into an "S" shape. But after that I decided to trust in God more.

While Mamma was in the hospital my sister Fajgi and I decided to surprise her by thoroughly cleaning our apartment. We emptied the ashes from our kitchen stove and we cooked a good, strong lye. Chasing our younger brothers out of the house, we carried in buckets of water from the backyard and we scrubbed the wooden floors in all five rooms. The floors turned a beautiful yellow, but the lye burned the skin off our hands, knees, and feet. It hurt terribly but we felt it was worth it. Our house was so sparkling clean, Mamma couldn't believe her eyes when she came home.

I loved Mamma ferociously and worried about losing her more than once. I remember one day, when I decided to investigate her possessions. My parents' bedroom had two large windows opening onto the street. Between the windows was a mirror and a dresser with a marble top. In the middle of the room stood a large table with four chairs around it. On one wall were two beds, and on the wall facing the beds, there were two armoires. I wanted to see what was kept in the armoires. I pulled up a chair to the one with shelves and opened it. It contained ironed sheets and pillowcases folded in perfect order. I went on searching. On one shelf, among some folded clothes, I found a large white dress and an envelope with a little bit of white earth in it. Curious, I brought it out and asked Mamma about it. She said it was the *tachrichem*. I knew what that was: the dress was the dress Mamma was going to be buried in, and the white powder was earth from Jerusalem to be sprinkled on her grave. I was disconsolate and cried for days. I thought Mamma was preparing to die. Finally Mamma noticed how sad I was and asked me what was wrong. I burst into tears as I told her. She hugged me and, laughing, explained that everybody prepared the tachrichem in advance to make sure that it was there when the time came but that she had no intention of dying just yet. I was tremendously relieved.

A Close Call

On Thursday nights Mamma started the leavening for bread, *chala,* and coffee cake. All the girls helped. We grated potatoes and sifted flour into a long kneading trough, carved from wood, for bread, a smaller wooden tub for chala, and an even smaller one for coffee cake. Early in the morning on Friday, we kneaded the different doughs and transferred the coffee cake to pans, and with Father's help, we took everything to Konstantinovitch, the baker. He divided the bread dough into loaves after we told him how many we wanted. He braided the chalas, assigned a number to each loaf of bread or chala, and gave us a copy of the numbers. At noon we returned with our numbers and two large baskets lined with tablecloths to claim and carry home our bread for the week. Usually it was Father, Fajgi, the little boys, and I who went to the bakery. On Friday afternoon some of us went back again with a pot of *cholent* which cooked in the baker's oven till Shabbos noon. This enabled us to have a hot noon meal every Shabbos without starting a fire. The bakery was on Kossuth Lajos Street, near the bridge.

Every two weeks Mrs. Stucz came to our house to do the big washing. It was my job to pump the water she used for rinsing from the backyard well. After I had pumped enough water into her big tub, Mrs. Stucz ordered me to help with

I helped with the rinsing

rinsing and bluing the clothes. At first I didn't know how to ring clothes. I held them in my right hand and tried to twist with my left hand. She told me, "That's not right," and she put the clothes in my left hand. It went much better that way. Later Mrs. Stucz made me help with the washing also. Mamma didn't mind, and I thought it was interesting. I learned to wash and, later, how to iron.

When the clothes were washed we put them into a large basket and Father carried them up to the attic. We had lines there to hang them on. I helped with the little pieces but Father did most of the hanging. We kept a long ladder by the attic door that was above our apartment. My brothers and I liked to hang on it and do gymnastics dangling from the rungs. Once Father went up the ladder with a big basket on his shoulders. At the attic opening, he put the basket inside and was about to step in when the ladder slid out from under him with a big bang. I was sitting in the doorway of our apartment on a little chair and the ladder's ends scraped my back. I jumped up screaming with pain, and then I saw Father hanging by his hands from the attic. I forgot about my pain and ran to get the neighbors to help. I was so afraid Father would fall that I was still screaming. After that, before embarking for the attic, Father always made sure that the ladder had not been moved from its correct position.

Neighbors, Gypsies, and a Dybbuk

By third grade, I was helping Mamma so much, I had very little time left to play. But I did talk over every event that affected our lives with the neighbor children. I was always curious about what everybody was doing. At about this time, the Gelbs, who lived next door to the Zusmans, moved away because their apartment, which had two rooms and a kitchen, was too small for them. I was sorry to see them go because they had children my age and the Loevingers who moved in had only two older boys. It turned out the Loevingers had their good points, too. They made hats and steam would roll out from their apartment at all hours. They had model heads of different shapes and sizes and they pulled and stretched the hot, steaming felt onto them. It was interesting to watch. They had a good trade because everybody wore hats.

•

Beyond the Loevingers' apartment, the veranda turned to the left. The next apartment on that side belonged to the Jaegers. Mr. Jaeger had thick white hair and no beard. Mrs. Jaeger had a fascinating double chin. They had two adult sons, Shimi and Gadel, and an adopted daughter named Etyu.

One day the gypsies came to town and a beautiful gypsy girl cast a spell on Gadel. At least that's what the neighbor children said had happened. The spell was so powerful,

Gypsies

Gadel couldn't live without the gypsy girl. Abandoning his family he joined up with the wandering gypsies. Poor Mrs. Jaeger cried and cried and Mr. Jaeger became a sad and embittered man.

After a long time, Gadel came home for some reason. We were playing in the courtyard when all of a sudden we became aware of arguing in the Jaegers' apartment. Mrs. Jaeger ran out, screaming, "Help, help, he is killing him!" Mr. Jaeger was trying to strangle Gadel. It took Father and several other neighbors to wrestle Mr. Jaeger down and free Gadel. After that Gadel never came back. If alive, he is surely still wandering with the gypsies.

On the right-hand stairway to the veranda, in the apartment beyond Mrs. Eisner's, there lived a rabbi, Ereb Abbis, and his family. His wife was thin and looked unhealthy. They had a daughter, who was rather plump. Ereb Abbis wore a long black coat, white stockings, and a *shtramli,* a hat made from thirteen sable tails. Many *chassids* came to his house. They were the most strictly observant ones in the whole building. When the daughter was about sixteen years old they married her off. The wedding ceremony took place in the yard. The guests all crowded around the *chuppa,* the wedding canopy. The men, dressed in black caftans and hats were on one side, the women in their holiday dresses on the other side. Everybody held a lighted candle. The *chazan* who sang most of the prayers had a beautiful voice. Especially honored guests sang some of the prayers. The *rebetzen* and the mother of the groom led the bride around the groom seven times under the chuppa. Then the groom crushed a glass under his foot and everybody shouted *"Mazel tov."* The courtyard echoed and the other neighbor children and I, who were watching the proceedings from the veranda, thought it was all great fun.

The son-in-law moved in with Ereb Abbis. Shortly after the wedding a terrible thing happened. A *dybbuk* moved into the body of the newly married young woman. She kept running out of the apartment naked or half dressed, singing, dancing, and talking nonsense. She would try to kiss everybody. She couldn't help it: she was possessed by a bad spirit.

The wedding

Famous rabbis and doctors arrived to chase away the dybbuk and free her, but nothing worked. Finally she ended up in the asylum in Sziget like Mrs. Adler.

A Death

In our building, those who lived upstairs with apartments opening from a veranda were wealthy compared to others whose apartments were between the outhouses and the wooden sheds. The Indigs and the Bleiers lived there. Mrs. Bleier, a widow, had three beautiful daughters—Etu, Rozsi, and Eva—and a son, Mechu. One day there was a big sensation in the building. Mechu was caught and arrested for burglary. Poor Mrs. Bleier, who was very religious, was terribly ashamed. Mamma went to console her and I went along. Tears in her eyes, Mrs. Bleier wondered how could God parcel out so much *tsores,* so much misery, to one person.

Not long after that Mrs. Bleier died. Her death upset

Mamma very much. She told all of us children that we had to go ask her forgiveness for anything we might have done to hurt her. We were scared, but we did as we were told. We knew that Mrs. Bleier's body had been washed and dressed in white. Her toe and finger nails were cut. She was lying on the kitchen floor on two planks of wood, covered with a white sheet, two candles burning at her head. Everybody was very solemn and sad. We said we were sorry if the noise we made while playing had bothered her. Four men picked up the planks and carried her to the cemetery where she was buried between six planks of rough wood which were not even nailed together.

While Mrs. Bleier's body lay in the apartment building, Father stayed across the street from our house because as a Cohen he was not permitted to remain in the same house with a dead body. Mamma sent me with food for him, and I could tell from his face that he too was very sad about Mrs. Bleier. When Mamma returned from the cemetery I heard her tell Father that poor Mrs. Bleier was barely forty years old. Father said that it was Mechu who put her in the grave. He had broken her heart. There were sixteen families in the building, and there was tsores everywhere.

The Holidays

Being Jewish was an all-pervasive fact of our existence. On weekends there was a military band at the park and we liked to go and listen. But on Saturdays we could go only after we had recited the Shachrit and Musaf Shmoneh Esrah (the standing prayers for Saturday morning). Mamma would sit and listen to each of us say it.

We looked forward to each religious festival. At Purim Mamma made all kinds of pastries and we kids took *shalech mones* (gifts of food) to all the neighbors and friends. Other families sent us their cookies. There was a friendly competition, everybody trying to outdo each other in making the best Purim sweets. The children dressed up in Purim costumes and went from house to house to say the Purim *spiel* (poem). After reciting the poems, we were given a little money at each home. Counting our money and anticipating how much more we were going to amass, we were happy and excited. The day before Purim, on Estertanes, kids fasted until noon, grownups until evening.

Before Pesach we went to watch the matzo baking in the cellar of the Jewish school on Vardomb Street. I can still smell the freshly baked matzo. To get ready for Pesach, we emptied the house of every piece of clothing and hung it on a large ladder in the backyard. We even put the *Machzur* and *Siderles* (everyday prayer book) out in the sun after going through it page by page to make sure there was no *chumayts* (leavened bread crumbs) stuck between the pages. We cleaned and cleaned and painted the walls before we brought down the Pesach dishes from the attic. When everything was clean, Father went from room to room with a feather duster and a wooden spoon to sweep up any last bit of chumayts he could find. It was unlikely that he could find any after all the cleaning we did, so we made sure to put some in obvious places. He took it outside and burned it while saying the appropriate prayer. Preparations for the *seder* kept all of us busy. I remember anticipating the ransom of the *afikoman*. The afikoman is a special piece of matzo, which is required for ending the seder. The kids were supposed to hide it and the adults were supposed to ransom it so that the seder could be ended. The purpose of this play acting was to keep the children interested, but I was so excited I always fell asleep with exhaustion before we got to the end.

To celebrate Shevuos, spring harvest, Mamma used flowers and walnut leaves to decorate the house. I can still smell the aroma of those walnut leaves.

In the fall, for Sukkos, Father built a *sukkah,* a symbolic booth, and covered it with reed leaves which he had cut from a patch on banks of the Szamos River. He had to go really far to get them. We all helped in decorating the booth. We painted walnuts gold and silver, made paper chains and Mogen David shapes and hung them, along with all kinds of fruit, from the ceiling of the sukkah. During Sukkos, the whole family ate in the sukkah.

During Chalamoyd, a half holiday that falls in the middle of the week during both Pesach and Sukkos, we played a game called Darg. Everyone built a little tower, called a *darg,* by putting a walnut on top of three others. Next we established an order of playing by seeing who could roll a walnut the furthest. Then we attacked the dargs, using a walnut as a projectile. On Chanuka, after Father lighted the candles, we played with wooden *dreidels* we had made ourselves.

The height of excitement came with the High Holy Days in the autumn. Mamma dressed all in white to go to temple. She wore a floor-length skirt with beautiful Madeira embroidery on it and straw shoes. Her tall figure hidden under voluminous skirts, her demeanor serious and festive, she was to my eyes the most beautiful being in the world. We went to the temple on Vardomb Street, the biggest one in town. During the High Holy Days, there were so many people there that policemen, dressed in holiday uniforms, stood in front of the big iron gates to control the crowds.

On Yom Kippur, Mamma and Father prayed from morning till night. The children all went to temple with Mamma. We were supposed to stay near her in the *waber shul,* the women's section.

I spent many hours there looking out through the wooden lattice at the men praying bellow. Wrapped in their prayer shawls, most of the time each man prayed at his own speed, occasionally standing up and swaying. The

The Waber shul

cantor would chant the last line of each prayer to make sure that they kept more or less together. There wasn't much to do for a child, so after a while we all ended up playing outside in the temple courtyard.

Zishu

My parents took great care to raise us as observant, orthodox Jews, and also to make sure that each of us had a trade. My brother Zishu, two years younger than Perl, was apprenticed to Mr. Boros, who owned a large print shop with a bookstore in front of the shop. He worked there for years, and I went there often to take him lunch. The print shop was on Ham Janos Street, next to the Victoria Hotel, across the street from the theater. The Boros family loved Zishu and I remember how happy Mamma was to hear Mr. Boros praise Zishu.

Zishu was very handsome. He was going out with girls and spending money on them. He often got into trouble with Father, who beat him with his belt, because he thought that Zishu was becoming too assimilated. After one beating, Zishu moved out. Without his pay, which had helped support the family, life became more difficult for the rest of us. At about the same time he completed his apprenticeship, but Mr. Boros didn't give him the pay raise he was promised. Zishu wanted to leave Mr. Boros and look for another job, but Mamma convinced him to stay on a while longer because his job was secure and it would have been hard to find another job in his trade in Szatmar.

Then in 1934, Feter Ancsel Duved, the husband of Mamma's step-sister who lived in Tasnad, proposed a shidech to Mamma between Zishu and his daughter Margit. She was a year younger than Zishu, who was twenty. She was a nice, industrious girl, and she would get a fifty-thousand-lei dowry. Mamma saw it as a very good idea because he was old enough to marry, and with the fifty thousand lei they could move to a different town where he would be able to find a job easily. Zishu agreed. They married and moved to Kolozsvar (Cluj) where they rented a small apartment. Zishu found a good job right away. They were good for each other and they learned to love each other. In 1936 they had a beautiful baby girl whom they named Eva.

Szimu

Szimu, two years younger than Zishu, had long, reddish-brown hair and a straight, imposing posture. She was the most beautiful girl in our family and also the most modern. She was the only one who had finished high school. She read a lot and she often gave me books to read. Father would get very angry. "It is not good for a religious girl to read novels," he would say, and if he caught us he would throw the book in the fire.

One day a *shadchen* came to propose a shidech for Szimu. The prospective husband, Jumi Tishler, was modern but religiously observant. According to the matchmaker he came from a good family. His parents had a candle factory, so they were obviously well off. He seemed to represent the ideal choice for Szimu, who would not have been happy married to a strictly orthodox man. And he was willing to accept a dowry of "only" fifty thousand lei. Mamma, of course, immediately said, "Let's look into it." Jumi was tall, good looking, and charming. He inspired so much confidence that Mamma agreed to the match without looking carefully into the matter any further. They set a wedding date making sure there was enough time for the dowry to arrive from America. In the meantime there were feverish wedding preparations. Mamma was happy that another of her daughters was getting married, and we all shared in her joy.

That summer, Fajgi and I went to camp. Camp was in a big house on Hunyadi Street, near the infantry barracks. The house had a huge backyard with large trees under which long tables with benches were set up for us. Inside the house was a big dining room where more tables and benches were lined up. Mr. Loevi, who lived there, was employed by the JOINT (the American Jewish Joint Distribution Committee) to administer the Jewish orphanage and to provide a summer day camp for the town's poor Jewish children. There were hundreds of children there in the summer for stints of ten days each. It was the best vacation I ever had. I made lots of new friends, ate good food, and had many new experiences. We made mud pies, sang songs, listened to stories. On Wednesday, dairy meal day, they gave us a cheese Danish for desert. One Wednesday I went to the huge kitchen after lunch and asked Bajcsu, Mr. Loevi's daughter, if I may have another cheese Danish because they were so very good. She looked at me, went to the great big baking pan, and, smiling, gave me another one. It was heavenly. I was sure I could have eaten two more, but I didn't ask.

One day at camp, an older girl came to talk to Fajgi and

me. She took us aside and said that she heard that our sister was about to marry Tishler. "Didn't our mother know that he is not a man to be trusted?" she said. We could hardly wait for the end of the day so that we could go home and tell Mamma. But when we told her, she barely listened to us. "Children's gossip," she said, and she dismissed it. She had too much invested already to believe us.

Preparations for the wedding went on. There was a lot of coming and going. Mamma cut off another piece from her big gold chain to pay for everything. She wanted to buy the newlyweds some furniture as a wedding present, but Tishler said he would prefer renting a furnished apartment for a while. The dowry arrived and the *chasene* took place. Tishler and Szimu moved to the furnished apartment, and Mamma had one less girl to worry about. Now there were only four of us girls left at home.

A short time after her wedding, Szimu told Mamma that her husband often left home at night and she had no idea where he went or what he did. Mamma tried to console her, but Szimu left crying. A few weeks later Szimu gave up the furnished apartment and moved back home. Tishler had disappeared.

Szimu's returning home bothered Father who felt that it was her fault that her husband had left her. He found fault with everything Szimu did. Szimu tried not to be home when Father was there. One day, Szimu was out on the veranda secretly smoking a cigarette when Father happened to come home unexpectedly. Busy hiding from Mamma, Szimu didn't notice him until it was too late. Seeing Szimu smoke infuriated Father. He dragged her inside, and, wrestling her to the ground on the threshold between the kitchen and the small room, he took off his belt and started to beat her with it. Sitting on a kitchen stool in front of the stove, Mamma begged Father to stop. Frightened, I was hugging Mamma from behind. Father wouldn't listen. I was crying and

Mamma was crying, but Father wouldn't stop. He beat Szimu so severely, I was sure that she would die right there on the floor. I never forgave Father for that beating. And I knew even then that I would never forget it. Szimu left home the next day and I never saw her again.

Father blamed Szimu's secular education for all her troubles and insisted that Hajcsu and Malku quit school immediately. Mamma took them out of school and apprenticed them to learn sewing. Their high school teacher came to our house to try to change Mamma's mind. They were both very good students, each having skipped a year already, and it wouldn't have taken them long to finish. But it was to no avail. Father didn't want them to finish high school.

Malku was apprenticed to Ilonka Szucs, the town's best shirt maker. She worked there seven years until she married. Soon there was no one in town who could make shirt collars as well as she. I don't remember where Hajcsu was apprenticed.

Szimu had gone to stay with a girl friend until she obtained a passport to Hungary. Then she went to Budapest where she found a job as a waitress. She had only a six-month visa, and she couldn't get an extension after it expired. Unwilling to come home, she wrote to Mamma that she was going to Arad, where she had landed a job at an orthodox, kosher restaurant that had just opened. She did well until fate intervened.

Szimu's husband Tishler was a con man. He had a partner, who posed as the sadchen, and proposed the match to Mamma. They went through the masquerade of marriage broker and groom only to get Szimu's dowry. When Tishler disappeared after a few weeks with Szimu's money, it was to practice his trade in another city. By chance, he had made his way to Arad, where he was caught and jailed at just about the time Szimu moved there. Reading about him in the paper, Szimu decided to go to his trial. It was there that she found out all about who her husband really was. In despair, she jumped off the third story of the courthouse. She didn't die, but she broke both of her feet. Her feet became infected and they had to be amputated. Szimu wouldn't hear of it. The doctors in the hospital told her that she would die of blood poisoning if she did not agree to the operation. She chose to die. She was barely twenty-one years old.

While all this was going on, Mamma was in Czechoslovakia, visiting her parents. It was Malku, four years younger than Szimu, who sat by her bed in the hospital. It was Malku who arranged the funeral at the orthodox cemetery in Arad. As a suicide, Szimu was buried near the cemetery wall. Malku was the only one at the funeral. Szimu was alone in a strange city and none of her friends or family knew what had happened.

Mamma stayed in Czechoslovakia for four weeks. She had my three younger brothers and my sister Fajgi with her. She never took me because I was always getting into trouble. When they got home, I was ecstatic to see them again. Mamma couldn't tell us enough about the wonderful time they had. My grandparents had taken them to the famous Karlsbad Springs, and she described how beautiful it was there. She told us that Grandma and Grandpa had a big, beautiful house with many servants. There were even peacocks in their front yard. She brought back presents—clothes and shoes, damask sheets and pillowcases, table cloths, and other gifts. She had brought me a beautiful pair of brown and beige patent leather shoes that, to my great disappointment, were too small. We had to sell them.

Malku didn't say anything to Mamma or anyone else about Szimu's death. She didn't want Mamma to have to sit *shiva*. To sit shiva is to sit on the floor and pray for seven days after the death. One does no work of any kind and one does not leave the house. It would have been very hard for Mamma to observe this custom with five young children in the house. When the time required for sitting shiva was over, Malku still couldn't bring herself to tell Mamma. Finally, after a long time she asked Ilonka Szucs, her employer, to break the news of Szimu's death to Mamma. It was only then that Malku told us details about how Szimu died and how much she suffered. Mamma and we children were frozen with pain and disbelief. When I write about it now, more than 50 years later, I still have tears in my eyes and my heart still aches for my beautiful, unlucky sister.

Bucium

When Perl had her second child, a boy, she wrote to Mamma asking if Fajgi or I could stay with her and help take care of the children. Mamma decided to send me. She thought I could go to school in Perl's village and still have time left over to help. She decided to send me because I was continuously fighting with my younger brothers. My brothers called me "Richu," which means devil, instead of Ruchcle. It made me angry to be called Richu, and since they kept calling me that, I had to keep on hitting them.

Once, exasperated by their incessant teasing, I decided to take revenge. They were always trading with and selling to the other children buttons, sweets, and candy. They kept their merchandise in the locked drawer of the mirrored dresser in my parents bedroom. But the drawer had a marble top that could be lifted up. I lifted the top, removed all the candy, and ate it. When they found out that I had robbed them, they tried to beat me, so I ran away.

When hunger drove me home, I approached the door carefully. They were hiding near the door, waiting for me with broomsticks. I saw them and I ran away again. The trouble was that Mrs. Freiman, a customer who wanted to buy meat, arrived at the same time. We usually had no customers after midmorning on Friday, and because she was small, the boys thought she was me. When she stepped inside the door they hit her on the head with the broomsticks.

Imagine the scandal! Attacking one of Mamma's customers! I was really worried about what would happen next. Mamma scolded the boys. She took out two goose legs and a few pieces of chicken from the soup cooking on the stove and gave it to Mrs. Freiman so that she wouldn't be left without a meal on Shabbos. After that Mrs. Freiman was ready to forgive the boys. She had fallen into my brothers' trap because she was two weeks behind with paying Mamma. Embarrassed to ask for credit again, she had hesitated until the last minute to buy her meat.

I felt really strange. The boys got scolded for attacking her, Mrs. Freiman got the beating that was coming to me, and I, who instigated the whole thing, wasn't even reprimanded. That seemed to be the end of the affair. But when we sat down for dinner that Friday night, my portion and those of my brothers were so small we could hardly see them. At first we threw them back with cries of "*Nor asoy fil* [Is this all]?" When we realized that was all there was and that we ourselves were to blame, we took our portions back sheepishly.

Another time, I decided that I wanted to be beautiful. I saw some of the older neighbor girls using make-up and thought I could get the same effect by improvising. There was a kind of candy which was wrapped in red paper. By rubbing the candy wrapper on my skin, I painted my face and lips. As a finishing touch I cut off my eyebrows. Poor Mamma couldn't believe her eyes when she saw me. I was always a handful.

Before Mamma sent me to Perl's at Bucium someone proposed a shidech for Hajcsu. The boy, Shulem Fried from Temesvar (Timisoara), wasn't very religious, but he had a trade. He was a tailor who made suits for peasants. Mamma had learned to be cautious. She hired someone to find out if everything we were told was true. When she had satisfied herself that everything was in order, the letter was sent off to America again, requesting a dowry for Hajcsu. And another piece of Mamma's golden chain was sold to pay for the wedding. I wasn't home for the wedding. I was already in Bucium helping to take care of Perl's children and going to school there.

In Bucium, Perl and Avrum's house was behind the village temple. The temple was a square, white-washed building taller than all the buildings near it. It had tall, narrow, arched windows, with sills at the height of a man. A round window, in the center of the front wall and higher than the other windows, had an inlaid Star of David, which advertised the purpose of the building. Above it was an arch in the wall.

The men entered the temple from the side through an entry hall, which was used as the cheder, the Hebrew school for the children. The hall was furnished with a long table with wooden benches on each side, and a chair on the end for the teacher who was called the *rebe*. On one side of the entry, on the wall next to the main door, stood a small bench holding a bucket of fresh water, and a copper cup with two handles. There was a bucket underneath the small bench for the dirty water, and a rough, hand-woven towel on a nail above the bench. On the far wall of the entry hall stood a tall, wood-burning stove to warm the room in the winter.

The ceiling of the entry hall was much lower than that of the rest of the building because above it was the woman's section of the temple, the *waber-shul*. The waber-shul, entered through a wooden staircase at the back of the building, consisted of benches facing a dense wooden lattice, through which the women could look out at the men praying below and at the eastern wall.

The sanctuary, reached through double doors from the entry hall, didn't have its own heating and during really se-

The Jewish temple in Bucium

vere winters the services were conducted in the cheder. On those days women did not attend. In the sanctuary at the center of the eastern wall stood a wooden ark, stained a walnut color. It contained the Torah scroll. The ark was covered with a heavy, red velvet curtain with golden yellow embroidery and fringes. A prayer stand for the *baal tefilah,* the person conducting the prayers, stood to the right of the ark. On the wall on each side of the ark were seats for the influential people of the village. Facing them a little distance away were the pews for the rest of the congregation. They were arranged around a pulpit in the center of the room that was used for the reading of the Torah scroll. The wooden pews and pulpit were also stained walnut. In the back of the room was a long table covered with a white tablecloth and flanked by benches. That was where the children sat who were too old to stay with their mother and too young to participate fully in the services.

A separate building behind Perl's house held a mikve with two long pools with greenish water that I found scary. Perhaps I am mistaken about it, but I don't think anybody ever used the mikve. I for one stayed away from it.

Perl's house was ensconced between the temple and the mikve. It was a small house with tiny windows, a tile roof, and whitewashed walls. Most of the peasant houses in the village had tall, pitched, straw-covered roofs. Most of the Jewish houses had tile roofs. Perl's house had two bedrooms and a kitchen. She also had a stable where they kept a buffalo for milk and a few chickens. At the very end of the lot, surrounded by a picket fence, was a small vegetable garden with a couple of fruit trees at the edge. A city girl, Perl didn't have a green thumb and she didn't really have time for gardening. Often, when I took the babies out to play in the grass, we could hear the children from the village study their weekly Torah portions in the cheder.

They read the *sedre* out loud, first saying a phrase in Hebrew and then the Yiddish translation: *"veatu (di) tetzave (zolst bafelen) es (di) kol israel (de kinder of Israel) vajitschi (zoln nemen) alechu (tsi dir), shemen (oil soch) ailbirten, kusiv (tzi stojsen), lamoer (tzi lachten) lahalaos (untzizenden) nair (de lacht) tumid (bastendig)..."* Many weekly sedres got imprinted on my brain in this way, without my having ever seen them or studied them.

I stayed at Bucium with Perl's family for months. Homesick, I cried every day and begged to be taken back home. I missed Mamma terribly. Finally, Perl gave in and took me home. There I found that Mamma's younger brother Isidor was staying with us. He had come to say goodbye because he was going to America. Uncle Moric had sent him money for the journey and a ticket for the ship. He had come to Romania from Czechoslovakia to spend a few days with us before he left. He was very handsome and looked a lot like Mamma.

Busy inspecting the things he brought from my grandparents, I listened to him and Mamma talk about Perl and Zishu and other family members. Hajcsu and Shulem were expecting their first child. They lived in Turc, a little village near Halmi. With the dowry they had bought a small house, two mountain parcels with grapevines, a sewing machine, and a season's worth of the pressed raw wool felt that Shulem used to make suits for Romanian peasants. They were well, but Hajcsu didn't like living in such a small village.

It was fall, canning time. Mamma, Uncle Isidor, and I went to the market together, and we bought half a cart of cabbages and two cases of apples to make sauerkraut. Mamma put up cabbage every fall, but this particular occasion became a special memory for me. Uncle Isidor helped shred the cabbage and stuff it into a big barrel. He worked with such good cheer that I decided then and there that I would always love him.

Mamma cried very hard when they said goodbye to each other. She knew that there was a good chance that they would never see each other again. In fact, though they wrote to each other often and his letters were always an occasion for joy, they never did meet again.

Mamma was the best cook in the world. She added apples to the sauerkraut as a special treat. In winter, we looked for the apples stuck between the cabbage in the icy barrel. Soaked in the sweet and sour sauerkraut and half frozen, they were delicious. She also canned black grapes in large pickle jars so that her children would have fruit in the winter. The grapes in the thick syrup tasted wonderful and had an indescribable aroma. I have never eaten or smelled anything like it since.

I often wonder how Mamma had the strength to work so much and care about so many things. I can still see her watering the red geraniums she kept under the windows that opened onto the veranda. With all the other things she had to do, she still found time to take care of flowers.

Secret Errands

Sometimes on Thursdays, Mamma woke me up very early in the morning and sent me on a secret errand. I was to take a live chicken and fresh eggs to the doorstep of the rabbi from Bixad, whom she admired. Mamma impressed upon me that it was very important that nobody see me come or go. We were doing a good deed, a *mitzvah,* but it had to be done secretly for it to be a true mitzvah. I had to pass the bread factory on the way there and the aroma of the freshly baked bread always made me hungry. It was usually still dark when I hurried home, proud of myself for having done the job well. I knew nobody had seen me.

Sometimes Mamma sent Fajgi, and once Fajgi didn't do the job as well as I. She met a man who knew her and asked her where she was going so early. Taken by surprise, she told him that she was doing a mitzvah, taking a gift to the rabbi's house. The man said, "Tell your Mamma she'd be doing a bigger mitzvah if she cooked it and fed it to you." Fajgi was upset she knew she should not have told him. When she got to the rabbi's house, the rebbetzin also saw her, and she asked her into the house and took her to the rabbi. The rabbi was sick. Very pale, he was lying in bed. He put his hand on her head and blessed her. When she came home and told Mamma all about it, Mamma said only, "Next time don't tell anybody where you are going, or why."

Turc

One afternoon I was playing a game called "Give me soldiers, King!" in the yard with the neighbor children. In this game two groups of kids, each with a king, form two lines holding hands and facing each other. Then one king says, "Give me soldiers, King!" and the other king says, "No, I won't." Then the first king says, "If you won't then I will tear!" and the second king says, "Tear if you can!" After this exchange, the first group runs for the weak link in the opposing chain. Those who are "torn off" have to change sides but there is an immediate rematch, with the second king asking for soldiers, and the first king saying no. The game goes on until one king gets all the soldiers. We had been playing for a while when I decided that I wanted to be king. The others wouldn't let me. Very angry, I told them that if they won't let me be king, I will never play with them again. Just then, Mamma called me in, and I never was able to play with them again.

Inside, Hajcsu's husband Shulem was waiting for me. He always came laden with cases of fruit from his orchards. This time he had come because Hajcsu had just given birth to twin boys and they needed help. I must have done a good job in Bucium caring for Perl's children, for now I had to move to Turc to watch Hajcsu's babies. It had been decided already. Mamma told me that I was to be a good girl. She told Shulem that he could spank me if I didn't behave. Had she known Shulem better she wouldn't have said that.

I packed up my few clothes and my school books. I was to go to school in Turc. We took the bus to Halmi. I was upset and the smell on the bus turned my stomach. The bus had to stop three times because I kept throwing up. From Halmi we had to go 18 more kilometers in a horse-drawn wagon to get to Turc.

Turc was a larger village than Bucium but it was like being in a different country. Most of the houses were painted blue. The people went around barefoot in picturesque attires: white linen or hemp shirts and blouses, full skirts, and wide-legged, almost skirt-like trousers. Blouses and shirts were held in place with colorful woven belts for the men and aprons for the woman. Shirts, blouses, trouser bottoms, skirts were all embroidered with colorful flower motifs. Each woman prepared and spun the hemp, wove the material, and did the needlework on every item of clothing worn by her and her family. To show off their industriousness, on Sundays the women wore several skirts, one on top of the other.

In the winter the peasants wore thick, hand-knitted socks and moccasins, long sheepskin capes with the furry side on the outside, and suits of a material they called *ciora*, a thick, grayish-white, wool felt decorated with narrow black strips along the seams and on the collar. The women wore short jackets of the same material over their skirts. Shulem specialized in sewing these garments and it kept him busy from early fall to late winter.

At Turc

The house Shulem and Hajcsu lived in was a tiny, low, whitewashed structure. It was dominated by a huge oven that took up half the kitchen and was used for cooking, baking, and heating. The two small bedrooms, which made up the rest of the house, shared the back wall of the oven, relying for heating on the heat absorbed through the wall.

I was tremendously unhappy in Turc. Shulem enrolled me in fourth grade but the school was not for me. In

Szatmar, we were reading books by fourth grade. Fourth-graders in Turc barely knew how to read. There was nothing for me to learn there. I went to school rarely and I had very little in common with the other kids, so I made no friends. I mourned the life I had left behind.

I remembered how King Carol had stopped at Szatmar. Our teacher took us to meet him at the train station. There was a huge crowd, the military band played, and all the important people from the town were there. Yoylish Teitelbaum, the town's chief rabbi, was there, surrounded by his Chassids. The king came out of the train and descended the steps. People shouted, "Long live the king!" Children clapped, Rav Yoylish bowed, and the king shook hands with him. The king would never have gone to Turc, even if there were a train. Had he visited Turc, the people wouldn't have known how to act, and the school children wouldn't have had the appropriate clothes. We had beautiful uniforms in the city—black smocks with a white collar and a red ribbon under the collar. We also had proper school bags. At Turc the kids came to school barefoot in shapeless cotton clothes, carrying little cotton bags on their shoulders. I went to school only occasionally when I wasn't too busy at home. But I was always very busy.

Shulem had a horse, a cow, geese and chickens, and two babies, and it was my job to take care of all of them. Every morning I had to let out the cow and the horse to graze with the herds, clean the barn, feed the geese and poultry, carry water home from the well, and chop wood from tree-sized logs and learn to milk the cow. In addition, I had to watch the two little boys all day.

Shulem and Hajcsu were engaged in various business schemes. Often they went across the Czech border at Nagy Tarna to smuggle in textiles, which cost less in Czechoslovakia. If the night was clear and the moon was bright they couldn't come back because the border guards would have caught them. So I was left alone with two babies and all that work all day and all night.

But being swamped by work, having no friends, and no school to look forward to was not all. In addition to all this, Shulem lorded it over me and beat me. The cow got into the neighbor's field and was kept hostage until Shulem paid for the damage. I got a beating. When the horse didn't come home with the herd one day, I got another beating. The next day, I met the herd on its way home and ran into it to get our horse. The horse kicked me and went on its way and I fell between the horses. I went home and discovered that our horse had walked home alone. I had tried to bring home the wrong horse. That day, I got a beating for not being there to let in the horse. When the geese flew to somebody else's field and caused damage, I got a beating. It wasn't fair: what was I supposed to do, fly after them?

Feeding the geese

Shulem enjoyed having absolute power over me, and Hajcsu never stood up for me. She was unhappy at being stuck in a small village. Glad to have me there to shoulder her responsibilities, she took every occasion to leave. She didn't want to see that Shulem was abusing me. Even when she was there, she did not interfere. After all, I had a reputation as a difficult child, and Shulem was just "disciplining" me.

The only time Hajcsu was kind to me, it ended up causing more trouble. She brought me a present from Czechoslovakia—an embroidery pattern and many colorful threads. One afternoon, after I was done with all my chores, I sat on the threshold of our house with my embroidery and the two eight-month-old babies, who were barely crawling. I was absorbed in my work when, all of a sudden, I heard a neighbor screaming. One of the boys had crawled into the street and a wagon with two spooked horses was hurtling down the street. There was nothing we could do. We just held our breath. Miraculously, the baby didn't get hurt at all. He was black from the dust, but that was all. When Shulem and my sister got home and found out what had happened, I got so brutal a beating that the neighbors had to take me out of Shulem's hands to save my life.

I decided I was going to commit suicide. I planned to use an ax which I hid under my bed. I was going to kill myself when everybody was asleep. But I fell asleep first and didn't wake up until morning. In the morning, upset that I had fallen asleep, I decided to try harder next evening. But night after night, I was too tired to wait for the others to fall asleep. I kept resolving to kill myself and I could never stay awake long enough to do it.

Once Hajcsu went to Szatmar to sell the things they bought in Czechoslovakia, and I stayed home with the kids and Shulem. When Hajcsu wasn't there, I slept in the big bed with the two kids. In the middle of the night Shulem woke me because the cow had escaped. I went looking for her behind the peasants' houses, running between the rows of corn and crying. Finally after a long time I heard the sound of her chewing in the distance and I found her. Shulem's beating had not been particularly brutal this time but I decided I couldn't take anymore.

In the morning, I dressed the two babies and went to Shulem's aunt's house, at the other end of the village. I told her that I had to go home to Mamma and that I would die if I didn't.

She must have believed me because she made arrangements for a wagon to take us to the bus station, and she gave me money for the bus ticket.

She hired a wagon

On the way home with the two babies, I was so busy I forgot my jacket on the bus. It was a jacket I liked a lot and the only one I had. I was upset about losing it.

I told Mamma all that had happened and she said that I would never have to go back there again and that Shulem would not be allowed to enter our house again. She only kept half her word—Shulem was her son-in-law, after all—but I didn't have to go back there. The worst period of my childhood was over.

I was home again but things weren't the same. When we were little, on warm summer days, Fajgi, a few of the neighbor kids, and I used to go to the Kossuth Garden, on the corner of Atila Street, across from the train station. The garden had huge old trees and large grassy areas. In the middle there was a lake and next to the lake was a hill with a restaurant on top. We would spread out the blankets we carried and place on top of them the basket of food Mamma had packed us. We would exhaust ourselves racing up and down the hill. Then after eating, we would lie on our backs next to each other, watching the clouds for hours. But now Fajgi was busy. When she turned thirteen, Mamma apprenticed her for three years to the sewing shop of Irenke Steimetz. After her apprenticeship she stayed on as an assistant. She was a good worker and gave all her wages to Mamma. She was also smart and serious and Mamma relied on her more and more, often taking her into her confidence.

Malku

In 1938 my sister Malku was seventeen and had finished her apprenticeship. She was making shirts in the town's best shop. With her earnings, she bought herself a sewing machine. She made herself dresses and she also brought work home. All the dresses she made for herself were short sleeved. She wouldn't listen to Mamma who kept telling her that short sleeves were not appropriate for the daughter of a religious family.

Then a shidech was proposed. The boy was Chaim Zafir, from Nagy Karoly. Religious, educated, quiet and refined, he came from a *balebatish* family. Malku liked him. Soon a wedding date was set and off went the letter to Uncle Moric in America.

Something must have gone wrong, for the money did not arrive and the wedding date was approaching. Chaim's family was not taking any chances and insisted on postponing the wedding until the dowry arrived. Mamma, worried that we might lose Chaim, begged them in vain not to postpone the wedding. There was a lot of anxiety. Malku cried. Mamma sent a telegram to America saying, "*Nicht Kein Nadn, Nicht Kein Chasene* [No dowry, no wedding]." Finally the money arrived, a new date was set, Mamma cut off another piece from her necklace, and we had the wedding at our apartment. All of my sisters and their families were there. I was pleased that there were so many of us.

It was already winter. I remember how Hajcsu, pregnant with her third child, ran out to the kitchen during the mitzvah dance with the bride. She sat on the sauerkraut barrel behind the kitchen door crying about how lucky Malku was to get a man like Chaim and how unlucky she herself was, stuck in a little village and married to a simple peasant boy. How could Mamma have done this to her? Having stayed with her and seen what her life was like, I knew exactly what she was talking about, and was very sorry for her.

Malku and Chaim moved into the room which used to be the store. Mamma furnished it for them beautifully. Chaim was very observant so Malku could not use any of her many short-sleeved dresses. She cut her hair and wore a wig, a *shaytl*, as orthodox women were expected to. Chaim turned out to be clever and capable with his hands. Malku taught him how to sew and they bought another sewing machine for him. They worked together but it was she who always made the collars. They had a lot of customers because their work was so excellent. They were happy with each other. Chaim was Mamma's favorite son-in-law. After a year they had a baby daughter and two years after that a son.

Doctor Klein

After every wedding Mamma was so exhausted that she passed out. This had happened on other occasions also, whenever she had too many things to worry about. She would lie on the floor unconscious, with her arms and legs twitching, sometimes for long periods of time while we stood around her crying. As usual, Father fetched Dr. Alfred Klein. Dr. Klein said it was just nerves. He gave her an injection after which, as always, she came to herself.

Father had to beg the doctor to come because we didn't have enough money to pay him. Then a solution was hit upon. I would go to the Kleins' house to answer the telephone while they went out for dinner. I started spending many evenings there. Soon they asked that I come over in the mornings also to help with the cleaning or to go to the baker for fresh bread and pastry. Next they asked me to serve food to their guests. They gave me a white apron to wear over my black school uniform. I, instead of the cook, brought in the platters of food. I was pretty and the cook was old and ugly. It seemed like my lot in life was to be an indentured servant. I had escaped from Turc, but in return for Mamma's "treatment" I had become Mrs. Klein's slave.

The Kleins were misers. Their house was filled with furniture imported from France and the finest things money could buy. In the backyard they had a two-bedroom house in which they kept their daughter's outgrown clothes, Mrs. Klein's belongings from her previous marriage, and other discards. Everything was kept under lock and key: the food pantry, the wood in the cellar, the drawers, the doors to the rooms, the closets. A long chain of keys hanging from her waist, Mrs. Klein oversaw everything. Every morning she gave the cook the ingredients for that day's meals and the wood she needed for cooking. Then she would lock everything up again. She was convinced that only her vigilance kept the world from stealing her blind.

It was in their house that I first ate *treyfe*. The cook, who loved me and was always trying to fatten me up, gave me some bacon. It tasted very good, so I decided to take half of it home to Mamma. She almost killed me when she saw it. Seeing the great wealth at Dr. Klein's and the great poverty at home, I once asked Mamma why she and Father had so many children if they couldn't support them. She just looked at me and didn't say a word.

Once Mrs. Klein made me remove the pieces of a very fine set of china with twenty-four place settings from a dining room closet one by one. She stood next to me watching me the whole time. Then she was called away for something, and, bored with picking up the plates one at a time, I removed the whole stack. Behind them was an envelope filled with a bundle of five hundred and one thousand lei bills. The temptation was too great to resist and the occasion too singular not to take advantage of it. I took a five-hundred-lei bill, hid it in my shoe, put the envelope back, and put the stack of dishes back in front of it. Then, I went on removing the dishes one by one as if nothing had happened. Mrs. Klein came back. When I came close to the end of the stack, she sent me out of the room so I wouldn't see what she was going to do. The envelope was obviously her stash of hidden money. A few minutes later she called me back and made me put the china back, one by one. While I was doing that, I kept wondering, what am I going to tell Mamma about where the money came from? I had no pangs of conscience over stealing it. I had been working for them for free for months. When I went home, I told Mamma I found the bill blowing in the wind. She could hardly believe how lucky I was but it never occurred to her that I had stolen it. She knew Mrs. Klein and knew that stealing from her would be impossible. And she had a hundred uses for the money.

Transylvania Is Returned to Hungary

One fall morning in 1939, Father went to fetch potable water from the Little Market well. On the way home some Iron Guardists (members of the Romanian Nazi Party) ripped out half of his beard. He came home all bloody, with the skin torn off his face. This happened during the government of ministers Goga and Cuza. In the months that followed we heard rumors of other disturbances. We were full of anxiety, but we didn't know the extent of anti-Jewish activities. In the early part of 1940, hundreds of Jewish store owners were massacred in the Jewish quarters of Bucharest by the Iron Guard. Thousands of Jews were killed in pogroms and "disturbances" in Chernovitz, Chisineu, Iasi, Dorohoi, and other cities. Encouraged by new anti-Jewish policies, university students who were Iron Guard sympathizers came from other cities to demonstrate in Szatmar.

Those were bad times, and they quickly became even worse when in 1940, the Hungarians marched into Transylvania and "returned" it to Hungary. Now we belonged to an enlarged Hungary, along with the Southern Slovak territories (A Felvidek), which had been annexed in 1938, and Sub-Carpathian Ruthenia, which had been annexed in 1939. One consequence of these moves was that a lot more Jews fell under Hungarian jurisdiction than ever before. By 1941, the official estimate was that there were 850,000 living in Hungary. And this number did not include German, Austrian, Czech, and Polish refugees.

We were living in Hungary but we didn't automatically become Hungarian citizens. We had to prove that we deserved to be Hungarian citizens, and if we succeeded in doing that, we became the target of anti-Jewish laws which Hungary had enacted as early as 1920. At first, the intention of these laws was to keep Jews from being "over-represented" in desirable positions. Jews could not hold certain jobs. A quota system dramatically reduced the number of Jewish university students. A law decided who was considered a Jew: a person who had Jewish parents was a Jew, even if he had converted.

These laws didn't pass unchallenged. One hundred and one veteran generals of the First World War petitioned the upper house of the Parliament on behalf of their Jewish combat comrades. They were opposed to unjust restrictions and discrimination against Jews. They demanded equal rights for Jewish veterans and their widows and orphans. They argued that Jews who fought for the country were certainly at least as good Magyars (Hungarians) as those who had never risked their lives. Other renowned Hungarian leaders also spoke out. All their protests were to no avail. The majority of the people regarded the laws as legitimate. They stayed on the books and were enforced.

In 1939, another "Jewish Law" was passed which called for stricter and quicker enforcement of the existing laws and established more restrictions. The number of Jewish students in the universities and institutions of higher education was further reduced. Jews were forbidden to own real estate, to hold public jobs, and to join the civil service. They could not own stores selling goods on which the government had a monopoly. There was a quota (*numerus clausus*) on the number of Jewish newsmen, artists, actors, pharmacists, and other professionals.

The trend kept up. By 1940, another "Jewish Law," following the Nazi German model completely eliminated Jews from participating in public life. It attached heavy penalties to mixed marriages, it established labor camps instead of military service for Jewish young men, and closed the border to Jewish refugees.

When Transylvania became part of Hungary in 1940, we became subject to these laws. In addition, new anti-Jewish Ordinances were passed. Jews living in Transylvania had to prove that they and their families had been Hungarian citizens, or had lived in Hungarian territories, for three generations. Those who couldn't prove their Hungarian origins as stipulated by the law were placed in internment camps or were expelled from the country. So the immediate effect of being "returned" to Hungary was that the whole Jewish population of Transylvania was on the road, searching the archives of the places where their grandparents or great-grandparents had once lived. Jews were used to being law abiding citizens so they tried to comply with the law. Besides, what else could we do?

One morning in 1941, Malku's husband, Chaim, was arrested on his way to the synagogue. Because he didn't have the papers proving that he was a Hungarian citizen, he was declared an alien and put in an internment camp at Kistarcsa. Malku was left alone with two small children. She spent her time trying to obtain papers for Chaim and crying from frustration and desperation.

Because of an ordinance that decreed quotas for Jewish workers in the trades, my brother Zishu lost his job as a printer in Kolozsvar. He, Margit, and their daughter Eva, now five, moved to Budapest, where it was easier to become invisible as a Jew and to get a job. They rented a small apartment. Zishu found a job in his profession, and Margit got a part-time job in a millinery shop.

Kistarcsa is near Budapest. At Malku's request, Zishu visited Chaim in Kistarcsa to take him food packages. Zishu wrote to us about conditions in the camp. Malku had more reason to cry.

Apprenticeship

In 1940 Fajgi was seventeen and I was fifteen. Mamma tried to talk Fajgi into an arranged marriage to a very religious boy. Fajgi objected with all her might. Not only didn't she want to marry a boy that religious, she didn't want to marry at all. Later another candidate was suggested, this time a modern boy, a tailor. When the marriage broker introduced the boy, he turned out to be on crutches, with a missing leg. Fajgi cried and carried on. She just wanted to be left alone and unmarried. She was very strong-willed and must have convinced Mamma, because there was no more talk of marriage after that. Fajgi got to stay at home and work and help Mamma.

In the meantime, Mamma decided it was time for me to learn a trade. We had relatives at Solyva, so she made arrangements there with a seamstress who made women's dresses. I was to learn the trade in eight months instead of three years. Mamma had a feeling that times were too turbulent to commit me to a three-year apprenticeship and she knew that I was quick to learn. Mamma paid the seamstress for my room and instruction. Since meals were not included, Mamma arranged a *taig essen* schedule for me. I was to eat with a different family each day of the week. On Monday I ate at the house of a distantly related childless couple who had a textile shop on the main street of Solyva. They had no children. I can't remember their names but I know that I was named Ruchele after the man's mother. They received me with love. The lady of the house gave me a red blouse with a large, round collar and told me how beautiful I looked in it. But I didn't like the collar so I never wore it. On Tuesday I ate at the house of a cousin of my father, a family also named Katz. Their children, a boy and a girl, were grown and married and on Wednesday and Thursday, I ate at each of their houses.

On Friday, I didn't eat lunch. I was supposed to eat dinner at the house of relatives of Mamma called Fisher, who had a clock shop. Friendly and warm, I liked their house best of all. But at the seamstress's, where I was working, Fridays were the busiest day of the week. We had to finish the weekly work before Shabbos, I had to run and deliver the dresses to the customers, and then I still had to clean and scrub the shop. Often, by the time I was finished with everything, it was so late that I had missed the Fisher's Shabbos dinner. Disappointed, I would listen through the window to the *zmirot*, the after-meal songs. I was ashamed to go in and sad to have missed a lovely Friday night dinner. I went to sleep back at the seamstress' house, with my stomach growling from hunger.

Another relative, Fajgi Frilich, of the Grunberg family, was also boarding with the Fishers so that she could go to high school in Solyva. Her mother was a second cousin of Mamma's. Fajgi's family owned a hotel in Voloc, a ski resort. She was beautiful, with reddish-blond hair, which she wore in two great ponytails. She had a sunny disposition and laughed easily. We became great friends.

When the eight-month apprenticeship was finished, Father's cousin walked with me to the house of Mime Sure Kalus, my father's only sister, in Frigyes Falva. A few days later, again a day's walk away by foot, someone took me from there to another village, Lucska. Lucska had been in Czechoslovakia, close to the Polish-Hungarian border, but recently it had become part of Hungary.

Two of my father's brothers, Feter Shie and Feter Moishe, lived in Lucska. Feter Shie was rich and had no children. Feter Moishe was poor and had many children. I stayed at Feter Shie's house until his wife, Mime Tobe, said to me, "Your mother knows nothing but how to make children." After that I didn't want to stay there another minute. I moved to Feter Moishe's house. They didn't have so many good things to eat but I liked it better there because there were lots of boys and girls my age. On Saturday afternoons, the young people of the village would get together at somebody's house. We talked and we sang Yiddish songs. A girl, Etu, who had a beautiful voice and a boy, Ari, were very much in love. I watched them with fascination. Even though I was a city girl in a small village, I was having a great time.

Shiu and Fajgi, Feter Moishe's children, and Burech, Mime Kalus's son, from Frigyes Falva, and some other girls often went to the Hotel Star in Munkács to dance. Claiming that I was too young at fifteen, they would not take me with them. I wanted to go with them very much, especially after listening to them talk about what a good time they had. I was really upset that they wouldn't take me.

God, when I think of those times.... There were so many young people living happily in that hidden little village. And there were such horrible things in store for us all.

It was in Lucska that I saw the first "expelled" Jewish families. There was a whole convoy of them escorted by the gendarmes. They were coming from the neighboring villages, with all their children and belongings piled in wagons. They had to leave their homes because they couldn't prove that they were Hungarian citizens. The gendarmes forced them over the Polish border and made sure they didn't come back. But Poland didn't want them either. They had no place to go. It was a sight that made me want to cry to heaven.

Before going home to Szatmar, I also visited Feter Hershel and Mamma's sister, Mime Elka, in Batyu. They had a big house with a huge garden. They also had lots of children, but they were living well. I remember my beautiful cousin, Peju, who helped me make a dress. On Saturday afternoon we sat and talked all afternoon, sitting on a blanket in the garden. I only spent a few days with them but I'll always remember them.

In Szatmar, I had many girlfriends who wanted my company. I was sixteen, always happy and smiling. I had good looks and a good figure. Without Mamma's knowledge, I went with my friends to dance school and to the strand by the River Szamos. I didn't own a bathing suit, but my friends brought one for me so I could be with them. We also went to meetings of the Mizrachi Organization. Mamma would have disapproved of that too if she had known. Mamma thought a religious girl had no business in a Zionist organization, but I liked singing Hebrew songs, dancing the *Hora*, and being friends with the young people there. My friends and I often met under the electric clock on the promenade, the most popular meeting place in Szatmar. We would stroll up and down the promenade a few times, sizing up the boys and checking out the display windows of the department stores.

The promenade, which was about thirty-five feet wide, was bordered by the oldest, most important buildings of the town. The most impressive building was the four-storied Panonia Hotel in the middle of the block. The hotel was an architectural wonder. Two stories higher than any of the other buildings on the promenade, it had shiny blue enamel tiles, a tremendous sloping roof, and gingerbread decorations of the same blue tile on the balconies. The hotel, almost half a block deep, was built over a passageway which linked the promenade to Rakolci Street. Along this passageway were various tiny shops and restaurants and the entrances to the hotel.

Alongside the hotel on both sides, also facing the promenade, were buildings boasting expensive clothing stores, a yardage store, and a coffee house, where the French pastries displayed in its windows could be bought. The upper stories of the buildings housed expensive apartments with large balconies overlooking the park. These buildings had narrow courtyards flanked by workshops, and, on the upper floors, distinguished tailor and dressmaker shops.

At the intersection of the passageway through the Panonia Hotel and Rakolci Street was the "big movie house." Its entrance was on Rakolci Street, but its box office faced the passageway. Adjacent to the movie house were a police station, a fire station, and an elementary school. The fire sta-

The center of Szatmar

tion had a tall, thin, red-brick watchtower. A person on the tower's balcony could see the entire city.

In the summer, iron garden tables with marble tops and iron chairs were placed in front of the hotel on the prom- enade and inside the passageway. The area claimed by the hotel was delineated by huge, potted ficus trees. People sat at the tables with large beer mugs or tiny coffee cups, and read newspapers or looked at the passersby. Inside the huge hotel lobby, obscured by thick cigarette and cigar smoke, young men played billiards, and old men, smoking like chimneys, played cards, drank bitter black coffee, and talked politics.

My friends and I never went inside the hotel, and we never sat at the tables. Only older people or people with money did that. When we tired of walking we crossed the yellow brick road and rested on the green and white benches in the park. We feasted our eyes on pathways of white pebbles; arbors covered with red, white, and pink climbing roses; rose trees tied to white stakes topped by colorful glass balls, which sparkled in the sun; rows of ornamental trees,

91

boxwood hedges, and strips of green lawn. There was a fountain in the middle of the park and I liked to sit near it and watch the water splashing in the pool.

On weekend afternoons, a military brass band dressed in beautiful parade uniforms played Strauss waltzes and marches from an elevated square on the south side of the park. On the east and west sides of the park, shiny, black-horse drawn carriages lined up, waiting for fares. On Sundays, people engaged them just for a trip around the park, but they were also the only mode of transportation for getting to the train station, or to places too far to walk to.

We Are Going to America

A lot of refugees from the part of Czechoslovakia that Hungary had annexed and from the part of Poland which had been occupied by the Germans in 1939 were passing through Szatmar on their way to Romania. They told terrible stories about executions and mass graves. Listening, our blood curdling, we refused to believe that such things could be true. But Mamma must have decided that there was enough truth in them to warrant some action. She wrote to her brother Moric in America asking him to help us leave the country and go to America. In a matter of weeks, Uncle Moric sent everyone in the family boat tickets and fare for the rest of the trip. He and his wife Zsenka must have worked tirelessly to get everything arranged so quickly.

We started to make preparations for the trip. My friends all envied me when I told them that we were going to America. My parents could not embark on such an adventure without first going to their Rabbi, Rav Yoylish Teitelbaum. Rav Yoylish had been the chief Rabbi of Szatmar since 1934. He had been installed after a bitter, six-year fight between different factions of the orthodox community, following the death of Rabbi Eliezer David Grunvald in 1928. I remember

Rav Yoylish's installation. It was done with great fanfare. He was brought from the train station in an open, horsedrawn carriage led by a military band. His followers and other townspeople, restrained by police cordons, lined the street all the way to his residence. Rav Yoylish talked my parents out of leaving. He convinced them that they ought to stay and trust in God's will. So, with the boat tickets in our hands, we stayed.

We were not the only ones. Rav Yoylish had a large group of followers who listened to him in all matters. There were many other Orthodox Jews who stayed in Szatmar, persuaded by Rav Yoylish that it was the right thing to do, and as a result perished.

Rav Yoylish himself was saved from the Holocaust in 1944. He, his family, and many other wealthy and influential Jews escaped on a special train which took them from Kolozsvar, through Bergen-Belsen, to Switzerland and from there to Eretz Israel. They were ransomed in exchange for an enormous amount of gold and jewelry through arrangements made by Rezso (Rudolph) Kastner with Eichman. Many people felt that by rescuing privileged Jews in exchange for enormous amounts of money, Kastner had collaborated with the Germans. He was shot in the street in front of his house in Israel in 1953. Rav Yoylish stayed in Eretz Israel till 1947. Before the war, he had taken a stand against Zionism, against the state of Israel, against the use of Hebrew as a spoken language, against *aliah* to Israel. His stay in Israel did not affect his views. In 1947 he immigrated to the USA and settled in Williamsburg, New York, where he established a Hassidic congregation and continued on in the same way as he had in Szatmar. He died in 1979 at the age of ninety-two.

I know that he could not have known what a fateful mistake it was to encourage his followers to stay in Szatmar in 1943. But I cannot find it in my heart to forgive him for it.

~ Part Two ~

WAR YEARS

Fajgi and I Go to Budapest

Because of the anti-Jewish measures, there were few opportunities for employment in Szatmar. But Zishu, who had moved to Budapest at the beginning of the fall of 1941, was doing well. So Mamma decided that Fajgi and I should go there, too. Zishu could keep an eye on us.

Mamma had to make sure that we started out looking respectable. She took Fajgi and me to the textile store on the Promenade to buy us material for winter coats. The owner gave Mamma a chair to sit on and they talked about rumors and news until we chose a beautiful blue woolen cloth. We then took it to a tailor who made each of us a coat with matching hats. I loved the whole process of getting ready for the trip. I liked to see how respectfully the owner of the shop treated Mamma; to have, for the first time in my life, a coat tailor-made for me; to tell my friends that I was going to Budapest.

Mamma, on the other hand, had a hard time letting go of us. She had hundreds of things to tell us: we shouldn't stay with Zishu, we should rent a furnished room right away, we shouldn't work on Shabbos, we shouldn't eat treyfe, we should be sure to visit Chaim at Kistarcsa. Though it pained her to send us off, she was already making plans for Szruli. As soon as we were settled enough to take care of Szruli, we were to tell her so she could send him, too. We sat and listened to her quietly.

All of a sudden she stood up and brought us a clean glass. She said, "You see this glass? It is clean. But every touch leaves a mark on it. You are going far away from home. You'll be among strangers. You may think that you can do anything since nobody will find out. But everything you do leaves a mark on you. Remember you are my daughters and stay true to who you are." I have always remembered her words. I remembered even while I was pretending to be somebody else in order to stay alive.

Work and the Union

In the last minute it was decided that Fajgi should leave for Budapest two weeks before me. She rented us lodgings with the superintendent at 29 Zichy Jeno Street. It was a one-bedroom apartment, but it also had a bathroom. Fajgi and I shared a bed, another girl slept in the other bed, and the super slept on a couch at the other end of the room. Her husband slept in the kitchen.

The day after I arrived I reported at the police precinct as Rozsi Katz. I was no longer Ruchele. Fajgi had become Fani. To obtain a work permit, I had to have an X-ray. When I was standing in front of the X-ray machine, the doctor yelled at me impatiently, "Don't you even know enough to stand facing the machine, not with your back to it?" Embarrassed because I was half naked and because I didn't understand why he was so irritated with me, I told him that I was indeed facing the machine. He didn't believe me. He turned on the light to convince himself and than exclaimed, "You are a complete situs inversus." My heart, circulatory system, and internal organs are all completely reversed, left to right. I was worried what this might mean, but he reassured me that it would cause no problem. It was just a very rare, one-chance-in-a-million occurrence.

I studied the want ads, looking for a job. There were many jobs for seamstresses. I was hired at the first place I tried at 33 Nep Szinhaz (Folk Theater) Street. The workshop was owned by Mrs. Burgheimer, a widow, and her daughter Edith. They had a big apartment with the shop in a room next to the kitchen. There were ten girls sewing pillow cases, sheets, and comforter covers for two big department stores, the Corvin and the Parizsi (Parisian).

Mrs. Burgheimer did the cutting on the dining room table. The finished items were ironed in the kitchen. Edith helped with the cutting and supervised the sewing, finishing, and shipping. She sat me down next to a button hole machine and showed me how to use it. In an hour I had it down pat. Edith praised me for being so quick and clever, so I tried even harder.

The other girls warned me not to work so fast because the girl who did the ironing had just quit, and if I could do the buttonholes fast enough to finish early, I would be made to do the ironing also. But I didn't listen to them, and, sure enough, I ended up having to do the ironing. The fumes from the coal iron often made me faint. When that happened, Edith and Mrs. Burgheimer always took care of me with affection. They often invited me to have lunch with them and occasionally, because I stayed late to iron, they gave me dinner also. I liked working there. Mrs. Burgheimer and Edith worked along with the rest of us from morning till night. And I really appreciated the fact that they cared about me. When they saw that my lunch always consisted of bread and marmalade, they made an arrangement with the JOINT to provide Fajgi and me with lunch every day. I bought a food carrier consisting of a set of stacked bowls and I went every day at noon to a kitchen near the Western Train Station to pick up our lunch. It took a considerable amount of time since the workshop was close to the Eastern Train Station. I had to make up the time after work.

Back at the workshop, I ate the lunch watching carefully the whole time to make sure that I left half for Fajgi to eat at home after work. Sometimes I was so hungry and the cooked food tasted so good that I ate it all. On those nights Fajgi was very angry with me. I told her that it wasn't fair that it was always I who went for the food and that if she went half the time, she'd see how hard it was to save it. But she wouldn't hear of it.

At first my biggest problem was that I had to work on Shabbos. But I decided I had no choice. Fajgi, who refused to work on Shabbos, had to look for a new job every week. Sometimes she didn't get one until the middle of the week and then she was fired again on Friday. If Mrs. Burgheimer, who was Jewish, wanted us to work on Shabbos, I knew there was no chance to hold down a job without working on Shabbos.

Later I had another problem. In the fall and winter it got dark early and I had to pass O Street on the way home. O Street was where the prostitutes waited for customers. In the dark I was often propositioned and followed by men. I was so frightened I didn't know how to get away fast enough. I told Mrs. Burgheimer that no other girl worked as late as I did and that I wanted to go home at the same time as the others, when it was still light outside, because I was afraid of crossing O Street in the dark. She saw the problem but wasn't going to settle for less work from me. We agreed that I would start earlier than the others so I could go home with them. The newest one there, I knew I was expected to work harder. I didn't think this arrangement was unfair.

The only time Mrs. Burgheimer and Edith took time off was when Edith's fiancé, Benci, came over. Benci, an army officer, was older than Edith, who was about twenty-five. He looked very serious. When he visited, there was no cutting in the dining room and no ironing in the kitchen. Mrs. Burgheimer and Edith were busy cooking and preparing the house as if for a holiday. Edith would laugh happily, anticipating his arrival, and she always cried after he left. I could tell that they were very much in love, but I thought it strange that a Jewish girl would have a Christian army officer for a fiancé. The Hungarian Army was fighting alongside the Germans, and the Germans were the enemies of the Jews.

I worked at Mrs. Burgheimer's for a year and a half. During this time I met many young people who also worked at sewing and tailor shops. They convinced me to go with them to a union meeting and I joined the union. At one union meeting they asked me where I worked and how many hours. When I told them that I worked twelve hours a day and what I was paid for it, they were incensed. They said I should quit immediately. They could get me a job working eight hours a day at higher pay.

I gave notice to the Burgheimers, but they didn't want to let me go. They asked my brother Zishu to convince me to stay. I remember being called over from the shop into their living room, and, to my surprise, there was Zishu, ordering me to stay because the Burgheimers were such nice people. I knew that they were nice people and my conscience was bothering me, but I wasn't going to stay. We parted on friendly terms, though.

I spent a lot of time at the union, where, along with other young people my age, I took part in the activities organized by the union. We went on excursions, played basketball and volleyball, and produced variety shows that we all participated in. On one occasion I recited the poems "Mother" and "Tell me what the worth of a life which...." by Atilla Joseph. The poems are about the spiritual exhaustion caused by grinding poverty. Thinking of Mamma and of the poverty my family was wrestling with, my tears fell as I recited. When I was finished I got thunderous applause.

I had a big circle of friends and everybody was glad to

have my company. On Sundays we would go picnicking to the surrounding mountains and parks. We played volleyball and other games against teams from other unions. I played right wing. At lunch time we all sat in a circle and laid out the food we had brought on a big blanket. There were cold cuts, sweet pastries, cheeses, and all sorts of delicious delicatessen food. My contribution was bread with marmalade. I couldn't afford anything else. After lunch we usually recited poems, read aloud, and exchanged books. Sometimes a union leader would hold an improvised meeting informing us of the union's stand on political issues. Union gatherings were illegal, and sometimes the police raided our meetings. We were told that if that happened, we should eat any leaflets that had been passed out, so that we could claim that we were simply young people on an outing. I also went with friends from the union to movies, theaters, and dance school. I loved to dance and I took so many boys with me that the dance school didn't charge me the entrance fee.

The union got me a job at a men's tailor shop where I worked eight hours a day for a much larger salary than I was paid by the Burgheimers'. My job was to make shoulder pads and sew them into the jackets. It was a much larger shop than the Burgheimers', with as many as forty people working there, both men and women. The owner, Mr. Kraus, and his twenty-two-year-old son Laci worked alongside us all day long.

I was making such good money that I was able to send some home and keep a little for myself. I bought myself material, a pigeon-gray wool, for a suit. When Fajgi saw it, she wanted a suit made from the same material, but she didn't have the money for it. To get material for her before they sold it all, we pawned my material and used that money and most of our week's wages. Then we had to work and skimp for a few more weeks for money to redeem my material and to pay for the sewing. When we finally got our suits ready, we had our pictures taken dressed up in our new suits to show our parents how well we were doing.

I visited Mrs. Burgheimer in my new suit. Though glad to see me, they were upset. Benci, Edith's fiancé, was at the Russian front. There were rumors of many soldiers killed in action, and of freezing and starving to death in the trenches.

We had sad news of our own from Mamma. Father was ill and couldn't work anymore. He now spent most of his time in bed. In the same letter she asked us to look for a job for Szruli, who was coming to join us. When Szruli arrived we apprenticed him to an upholsterer. We both contributed toward meeting his expenses because he was not earning any money yet.

I worked hard at the Kraus's shop, not even raising my eyes from my work. Surrounded by steam from the irons, I wouldn't have seen anything even if I had looked up. I was too busy to notice that Laci, the owner's son, spent the whole day watching me. This went on for days and everybody else saw it and was amused. One day, during lunch, Laci invited me to his parents' summer house at Siófok for the weekend. I asked him if his parents would be there too, and when he said yes, I accepted the invitation. I spent a very pleasant weekend with them. I liked Laci's parents. I remember sitting with them in the garden and talking about everything under the sun. In the evening I thanked them for their hospitality and Laci walked me home. After that I went to a few parties and teas with Laci and met some other middle-class boys and girls. I became friendly with some of them but the truth was that I enjoyed the company of young people of the same social class as myself much more. I found Laci uninteresting. I told him that I didn't want a boyfriend, but he wouldn't give up. Finally I had to leave my job to get away from him.

Through the union I got a job at an even larger shop, called the Tailor Union Shop, which employed about 250 people. It was located on 29 Nep Szinhaz (Folk Theater) Street. The owner, Mr. Gutman, worked in the office behind the workshop. The shop was run by Mr. Klemencsics, the chief tailor. Mr. Klemencsics was a big, well-built, jovial man, in his late fifties. He was always in a good mood and this made the shop a pleasant place to work.

He loved to eat. His lunch was a ritual, almost as enjoyable to an onlooker as for him. He sat down at one end of the cutting table, spread out a large, clean white napkin, then set the food on the napkin and proceeded to eat with gusto. His wife would often send him a hot lunch with his daughter, a twenty-five-year-old, good-looking, although slightly overweight, blue-eyed blonde. I was always happy to see her arrive. Mrs. Klemencsics was a terrific cook and she always sent some delicious pastries for dessert which Mr. Klemencsics shared with me and two other girls who worked there, Gyongyi and Maria Kirtag. Mrs. Klemencsics must have known of her husband's habit because there was always plenty for all of us.

Mr. Klemencsics called us his daughters. Gyongyi set up the materials for cutting with a folding machine. Maria and I sewed the stiff cotton in the front of the suit jackets. Gyongyi was the same age as I, Maria was a couple of years older. I had met and befriended Maria at a union meeting before I started working with her. Pleasant looking, plump, and blonde, Maria was the mothering type. She needed someone to take care of and I didn't mind at all having her fuss over me. She came from a small town near Budapest. Her father was a postal clerk and her mother a seamstress. She had a younger sister my age named Ilona. Maria used to talk to me about her younger sister, mostly to muse how different they were from each other.

Maria was a good, conscientious worker and a committed union member, and she despised the Hungarian Nazis. Her sister Ilona associated with the rightist youth of their town.

She had gone to Germany, against her parents' explicit objections, on a scholarship obtained though a Nazi youth organization. She was studying drama at a theater academy in Berlin. As it turned out, knowing these facts about Maria's sister and knowing Maria and Mr. Klemencsics were instrumental in my surviving the war.

The shop hired a young man, giving him a seat next to me. When he learned I was Jewish, he asked if I knew Yiddish. When I told him yes, he told me a terrible story in Yiddish. He was from Poland, from a little town near Podolksz. At the end of August 1941 the Germans herded together the entire Jewish population of the region and slaughtered them. As far as he knew, he and another boy his age had been the only ones to escape. He had told the Jewish Council in Budapest what had happened, but they didn't believe him. I didn't want to believe him either, but his story was frightening and depressing.

At Home for the Last Time, December 1943

The whole time I was working I was sending money home. But I was also able to save up a little money, and during the Christmas break in 1943, I decided to spend it on a visit home. I hadn't seen my family in two-and-a-half years. I bought a black sweater for Mamma, thermal underwear for Father, and small gifts for my two younger brothers. I left on December 23 and arrived home in the evening. I was happy and excited to see everybody. My younger brothers were now fourteen and twelve.

Father couldn't get out of bed. He had lost a lot of weight. His yellowish skin was almost transparent. His eyes were large and sunken, and they shone when he looked at me. It was sad to look at him. I was strong and healthy, and my father, who had always been big and strong and busy working, was too weak to get out of bed. Mamma said there was nothing specific wrong with him. He had worked so hard all his life, he was suffering from exhaustion. He wasn't old, he was just very tired.

Mamma couldn't have enough of me. She kept looking at me and telling me, "*Shafele*, my little lamb, you have become so beautiful. You look just like I did at your age. You even have my nature—fierce and fearless." She always added, "*Ken ayen'hore* [Let not the evil eye see you]." She kissed and petted me and asked God to keep me healthy and to give me luck.

I saw Malku and her two beautiful children. Her daughter was already five, her son three. Chaim, Malku's husband, was still at Kistarcsa in the internment camp. Fajgi and I had visited him many times, taking food to him whenever we could. I told Malku that, given the conditions he was in, he was doing pretty well. Poor Malku cried hard when she heard about Chaim. I also told them about Fajgi, Zishu, and little Eva, who was already six, and Szruli. I had skimped and sacrificed to save the money for the visit, but I felt it was worth all the money in the world to be with them. I didn't know then that I would never see any of them again.

The days went by very quickly, and soon it was time to go. Mamma baked pastry to send back with me. I sat down next to Daddy's bed. Not saying anything, he just looked at me with his big, tired eyes. I bent down and kissed his hand. I didn't hug him: he expected respect, not familiarity. How I wish now that I had hugged him instead!

I left for Budapest on December 31. The train seemed empty. The only person I saw throughout the trip was the conductor passing through the wagon. Leaving my compartment, I leaned out the passageway window into the cool air. For a moment I thought of all my friends in Budapest and wondered where they were spending New Year's Eve. Then my thoughts wandered back to the last few days at home and to Mamma. We had stayed up talking every night till daybreak. She had told me that Perl and Avrum had moved from Bucium to Somkut, where he had found a better job. They now had four children, the oldest of whom was twelve. Hajcsu and Shulem had two more children after the twins. And Malku, who was finally able to find papers proving that Chaim was not a foreigner, was preparing to come to Budapest for an audience at the Interior Ministry. It was good that Mamma and Malku were together, especially now that Daddy was sick. Mamma was still selling goose meat, though it must have been hard for her to do it all alone in addition to caring for Malku's children so that Malku could sew.

Then my thoughts wandered on to the one bad moment we had the whole week. Mamma had talked to Mrs. Gitcse, a second cousin of Father whom Mamma didn't like because she always brought bad news. She was the one who had told us that Tishler had been arrested in Arad. This time Mrs. Gitcse had incomprehensible news. Her oldest son, Mayer, who had escaped from Poland, told stories of Jewish people forced into ghettos and then slaughtered or sent to death camps, which swallowed hundreds of thousands. "Could this be true?" Mamma wondered. "Don't you think that it must be false? After all, this is the twentieth century, and the Germans are civilized people!" She had already decided not to believe it. I had not wanted to believe the boy who sat next to me at work when he told me similar stories in his broken Hungarian and funny Polish Yiddish. But now I wasn't sure. Perhaps it was true. But it could not happen here in Hungary! Or could it? What did Mamma really think? Before I left, as we were crying and saying our goodbyes, she took off her diamond ring for me to give to Fajgi, and she put what was left of her long gold chain around my neck. Those were the last valuables she had. Did she believe those stories after all? Why else would she have given me those things?

The train sped through the cold winter night. Every turn

of the wheels was taking me further away from home. I returned to my seat, dried my tears, and tried to fall asleep. No sleep came. I sat watching the snowy fields and the telegraph poles racing by the window. Once in a while the engine's whistle broke the rhythmic clanking of the wheels. We passed an occasional guardhouse or a lighted station. Once in a while the train would stop at a deserted station and then run further into the night. I felt utterly alone.

I arrived at Budapest the next day at noon. It was New Year's Day and Fajgi was at home waiting for me with a hundred questions. I couldn't tell her enough about home. That same day, we visited Chaim at Kistarcsa to tell him that Malku had succeeded in finding papers for him and was coming shortly. In the evening we also went to see Zishu and his family. I took each of them some of Mamma's pastries and reported all the news from home. Little Eva sat in my lap eating the homemade pastries, her two big eyes glued on me. Then she chatted about how soon she would know how to write and then she would write to Grandma Ester.

A lot had happened in the week I'd been gone. Zishu had received his draft notice. He had to report for labor service in twenty-four hours. Margit had decided to take Eva to her parents in Tasnad until spring, so she could work more. Huge anti-Jewish posters had appeared on every street corner. Featuring grotesque caricatures of Jews, they said something like:

LONG-NOSED, BEARDED TYPES, ORIGINALLY FROM TARNOPOL, BRING DANGER UPON OUR HOMELAND

or:

THE JEWS INVENTED BOLSHEVISM. THEY ARE A DANGER TO THE HUNGARIAN PEOPLE, AND TO THE WHOLE WORLD.

At a union meeting, we decided to tear off or paint over such posters. We walked the streets at night carrying buckets of paint. Many were arrested, and in the end the union was banned.

I visited Mrs. Burgheimer, who had a radio and listened to the foreign newscasts. She assured me that the war was almost over and that the world would return to sanity very soon. But she was wrong. On March 19, 1944, the Germans marched into Budapest in a large parade. Prime Minister Kallay and his government stepped down, and they were succeeded by the Stolyai government. The papers were full of praise for the new era that Prime Minister Stolyai would usher in.

We decided to tear off or paint over the posters.

The immediate manifestation of this new era was the promulgation of more anti-Jewish measures. We had barely recovered from the shock of one measure when new ones were decreed. Jews had to turn in immediately to the government all radios, telephones, and cars that they owned. Younger and younger Jewish boys were being called up for labor service, sometimes with only twenty-four hours' notice.

Because restrictions on travel by Jews were multiplying daily, Gyongyi, my co-worker, was called home by her parents, who wanted her to be with them. Mr. Klemencsics hugged and kissed her when he said goodbye to her. He was really sorry to see her go. He gave me her job of setting up materials for cutting.

German soldiers march into Budapest

One day early in April, three SS officers came to the shop. When the boy from Poland saw them he got up and left without a word. He never came back. The SS officers went straight to the office of Mr. Gutman, the owner, and they called in Mr. Klemencsics. Then a short time later they walked out, pushing along a deathly pale Mr. Gutman, and announced that the shop no longer belonged to him. They took Mr. Gutman away, and he was never seen again.

From my circle of friends, more boys were called into labor service. It was the turn of the twenty-year-olds, and since so many were leaving at the same time, we decided to give them a farewell tea at the Astoria Hotel. The orchestra was playing "The Whole World Lasts Only a Day" by Karadi Katalin and I was dancing when I overheard someone remarking, "Look at that Katz girl dancing, and her father is barely cold in his grave." I wasn't sure I had heard right, so I walked over and asked him to repeat what he had said. He had just come from Szatmar, was well acquainted with my family, and knew for a fact that my father had died just a few days earlier. "Don't you know?" he asked me.

I felt like someone had hit me in the head. How could this be true? Why hadn't Mamma written? I left without even saying good-bye to my friends. One of the boys, Erno Hollander, insisted on walking me home. He said there was something very important he wanted to discuss with me before he left for labor service. Crying, I begged him not to talk to me about anything just then. He said he was sorry, but he was leaving the next evening, and he had to talk to me before he left. I agreed to meet him the next day after work.

I ran to tell the news to Fajgi. We sent a telegram home that same evening saying that we were returning home as soon as we could. The next day, I went to work while Fajgi made arrangements for our trip.

Erno Hollander met me after work. He told me he wanted to marry me after the war. He wanted me to write to him and to wait for him. He had been trying to tell me that he loved me for a long time, but I was always surrounded by so many other boys and girls that he never had a chance. He wanted my parents' address, so he could go there and ask for my hand at the first possible occasion. He knew that times were uncertain, but he for his part was certain that what he wanted from the future was to spend his life with me. He kept repeating how much he loved me. By the time we got to my house, I felt so sorry for him I promised to write him and wait for him. He told me he had tried to get me an engagement ring but couldn't. He asked me to accept instead a little golden necklace with a heart on it. I put it on. He hugged me and kissed me on the mouth. I drew away. It was the first time in my life somebody had kissed me like that, and I didn't like it. He told me again how much he loved me. Then he left to catch his train to report for labor service.

Fajgi had found that we could not leave the city. It was one of the new anti-Jewish measures. We asked the Jewish Council to help us to get a permit to leave. We waited there all day and then they told us to come back the next day. They themselves couldn't believe that we couldn't get an exception in a case of death. In the meantime we got a telegram from Mamma: "Father not dead. *Kumts nisht in fayer aryn* [don't come into the fire]." We didn't know what to think, but since Mamma didn't want us to return home and leaving seemed impossible, we resigned ourselves to staying.

Yellow Stars

A new decree was announced: all Jews had to sew yellow stars to their street clothing on pain of severe punishment for noncompliance. We sewed on the yellow stars and tried to go on with our everyday lives. It wasn't easy; the world was getting crazier every day. Newspapers in front-page articles accused Jews of signaling to enemy airplanes by putting shiny objects or white sheets on rooftops. Many Jews were arrested, tortured, and executed as spies.

Another new law was passed. The authorities designated certain buildings with stars. They evicted thousands of Jews from their homes and forced them to move into the starred houses. They didn't evict the non-Jewish people who already lived in the starred houses, so while the houses did not become ghettos, there wasn't much room in them. At first families occupied entire apartments and were able to take some of their belongings along. Later, there were six or seven families in a room, and people only took the barest necessities because there was no room for anything else. Fajgi moved into a starred house at 69 Nep Szinhaz Street, which was close to the place where she worked. She figured the less time she had to spend in public, the safer she was. I moved to 1 Klauzal Terrace. Szruli had just gotten an apartment in a building where no one knew he was Jewish, and he refused to leave it for a starred house. I figured it was okay, but I made Szruli quit the upholstery shop and through friends got him a job at a bakery on Vilmos Czaszar Street. That way he wouldn't have to worry about getting enough to eat and he could live from the little money he made even if we couldn't help him. Later he would crawl on his stomach during the air raids to bring bread to Fajgi and me.

Eva's Trip

I visited Margit. She was packing in order to move to a starred house at 20 Katona Jozsef Street. I was surprised to see little Eva there. Margit told me she herself could hardly believe it. Eva had been staying with Margit's parents in Tasnad. Margit's parents, unable to prove that their family had lived in Hungary for three generations, had been forced to move. Not wanting to take Eva with them to an internment camp, they had left her with neighbors and telegrammed Margit to come and get her. But Margit couldn't get permission to leave Budapest. In the meantime the neighbors, who had been ordered to move to the ghetto immediately, took Eva to the rabbi, who had a few days left before he had to move. He had sent word to Margit to come for her immediately, for once in the ghetto it would have been very difficult to get Eva out again. But Margit was still unable to get a permit to leave Budapest. Desperately, she had sent a telegram to Zishu asking him to try to reach Eva.

After much begging, Zishu was able to get a leave for two days and a traveling permit from his superior at the labor camp. He found Eva at Tasnad, but with his papers he couldn't buy her a train ticket. One had to show identification papers to buy a ticket. His papers identified him as Jewish, and Jews could not travel on the trains. He asked a sympathetic-looking peasant woman who had a child with her to help him. He explained his situation to her and told her, "I see you have a child. Here is my child and I love her just as much as you love your child. Please help me get her to her mother." He was lucky. The typical middle-class city-dweller would have turned him in. The simple peasant woman had not absorbed the Nazi propaganda spewed in the cities. She agreed to buy the ticket for Eva and to pretend that Eva was traveling with her. Worried that he himself would not make it to Budapest, Zishu explained to the six-year-old Eva that she was to sit next to the peasant woman, she was not to tell anybody that she was Jewish, and she should not let on that he was her father. He kept an eye on her from afar. He was rattled to the bone when the woman attracted the amorous attentions of an Arrow Cross goon, one of the Hungarian Nazis. It was a miracle that they arrived in Budapest without being asked to identify themselves even once. Zishu made it back to his labor camp safely. He had spent forty-eight hours traveling on trains, which were off limits for Jews, with papers clearly identifying him as a Jew.

Letters from Mamma

I got a postcard from Mamma in which she wrote that they had moved to Bathori Street. Chaim had been allowed to go home from the internment camp in Kistarcsa, and he and

Malku and Mamma and all the kids were sharing a room. All the other neighbors had moved too and were living in rooms near them. Before they moved, Erno Hollander from Beregsszaz, who was on his way to a labor camp, had paid a visit. He had asked Mamma for my hand. I thought the letter was strange. It didn't sound like her, the details she provided didn't add up, and important things were not explained. She didn't explain why they had moved nor why they now lived in only one room. The card had the word "censored" stamped on it in big red letters, but I still didn't realize that they were all inside a ghetto.

In May, another letter arrived from Mamma which she was able to sneak past the censor. It made us weep. She wrote that Father had indeed died about four weeks earlier. She wrote that he was probably lucky to have died when he did because at least he was resting in peace and didn't have to suffer the misery they were going through. She told us to stay where we were and not to even dream of going home. And she asked us to send them food. We asked Fajgi's landlady for a loan and sent a package the next day. We were happy that we were able to send it right away. We found out after the war that they never received it. We also found out that she had written to Zishu at his labor camp asking for food. She had written him, "Son, I worked for you for a lifetime. Now you must help us." It still makes me weep when I think of how desperate she must have been to write like that.

We received one more postcard from Mamma, postmarked from a place called Waldsee. It said only that they were all together and that they were fine. Fajgi and I couldn't find Waldsee on the map. Mr. Klemencsics promised to find out where it was. The next day he told me it was a resort town in Austria. We felt reassured. How could something bad happen to them in a resort town? That was the last we heard from them.

Many others received such cards from their families. Or

even more mysterious-sounding cards saying only, "I [in the singular, even though it was known that the whole family had been deported] have arrived. I am fine." The SS had people write them before they were sent to the gas chambers.

Laci Vamos

I became a close friend of Laci Vamos, an acquaintance of Laci Kraus, the son of the boss in my second workplace. Laci Vamos was from Nagyvarad (Oradea), which, like the rest of Transylvania, had been annexed to Hungary in the spring of 1940. In Nagyvarad, his father had a fur salon with a Christian partner. The partner was an honest man. He had learned that Jews would not be allowed to own businesses and would be forced to move into ghettos before the decree was announced publicly. Even though he had only to wait for the business to become entirely his through expropriation, he bought the Vamos's interest in the business and helped them leave Nagyvarad. They moved to Buda and bought a condominium there, thinking that owning a residence in Budapest would provide them with security.

Laci wanted me to meet his family. I visited them and became friendly with his sister Duci. One day, his mom told me in tears that Laci and I were spending too much time together, and that I should leave him alone. I was shocked. I had thought she liked me, and now it seemed she didn't. In addition, I considered myself engaged to Erno Hollander, and I thought that it was understood on all sides that Laci and I were just friends. I put it down to the fact that I was poor and they were rich. I excused myself and said goodbye. Angry with his mom, Laci told her that he was leaving home if I wasn't welcome there, and walked me home. We were lingering in front of my building talking when I saw my sister Fajgi coming towards us with Laci's father. Mr. Vamos begged Laci to go home and to have more patience with his mother. Laci wouldn't hear of it. Then his father handed him his notice to report to labor service in forty-eight hours. Now I understood why his mother was so upset, why she begrudged the time he was spending with me.

The next day Laci offered me an engagement ring. I reminded him that I was already engaged and told him that I considered him my friend. He insisted that we were more than friends. I didn't accept his ring but promised I would write to him. He left the next day.

When his first letter arrived, he wrote that he hadn't written to his parents and would not write to them because they had been mean to me. I wrote back to him that if he didn't write to his parents, I wouldn't reply to his letters. In his next letter to me he wrote a few lines to his parents and insisted that this was the only way in which he would communicate with them. He stuck to his word and kept me busy sharing mail with his parents. One day his mother offered me some cherries and said I should write to Laci that we are eating cherries from the same bowl. In Hungarian, "they are eating cherries from the same bowl" is an expression that means that people are really close to each other. I did write to Laci that his family had been friendly to me and that there was no need for him to act like a spoiled child. But having discovered a way to ensure that we stayed in contact, he stuck obstinately to writing his family through me.

Once, when I was delivering one of his letters, I found Duci and Mrs. Vamos crying. Mr. Vamos had been picked up by the SS, and they had no idea whether he was dead or alive. Without meaning to, I compared their situation to mine. They were full of anxiety, but they were at home, surrounded by their possessions, and they had each other to share their worries. My home and my mother had been beyond my reach for years. And by now I hadn't heard a word from Mamma for months. Crying, I said something to that effect. It sounded mean, but instead of taking offense they responded generously. They said that their home was my home too, and they considered themselves my family. Through his childish stubbornness, Laci had gotten his family to really accept me.

I corresponded with both Laci Vamos and Erno Hollander for a long time. Laci survived the war, but I did not marry him. He committed suicide in 1946. Although by that time he had married someone else, his mother blamed me for his suicide.

Erno had stopped writing after a while. His last letter came from the Ukraine, which, as I found out after the war, was a hell hole. His unit, along with many other units from Hungary, had been transferred to Bori, in Serbia. Bori became even more notorious than the Ukraine. Those who did labor service there were made to do hard labor building roads for the army or work in copper mines and rock quarries. They were starved, and much of the work was intentional torture by extremely cruel Hungarian guards. Weakened from hunger and living in unsanitary conditions, many came down with typhus. Those who were sick were separated from the others. They slept together on some dirty straw in a barn. One night, the guards surrounded the barn and set it on fire. Those who were strong enough to attempt escape were shot. The rest were burned alive. Few of those who had been sent to either Ukraine or Bori returned alive. Erno, who had been determined that we would marry after the war, did not.

Rooster-Feathered Gendarmes

One afternoon on the way home from work I met Kati, a girl I knew from Laci Kraus's group of friends. Happy to see me, she asked me a favor. She wanted me to go with her on the coming weekend to see her boyfriend, whose labor service unit was on the outskirts of Budapest, on Kerepesi Street. We agreed to meet at her house on Sunday.

Kati was the only child of well-to-do parents. Her mother prepared a package of food for Kati's boyfriend, and we were off. It was a beautiful summer day. Changing trams three times, we finally reached the outskirts of the city, where barracks full of men in the labor service lined the road. Kati's boyfriend and another boy were waiting for us at the gate. They must have paid off the guards, because we had no trouble entering the camp.

We entered an empty barrack and Kati disappeared with her friend while I stayed and talked with the other boy. When we said goodbye, he asked me to visit again. When we returned next Sunday, Kati disappeared again with her boyfriend, and my new friend tried to grab and kiss me. Surprised and annoyed, I left the barrack. He followed me and called my name, but I didn't turn around. I waited for Kati outside on the street, where he couldn't chase me. On the way home on the tram, Kati told me that she was afraid she was pregnant. That is when I realized that Kati was intimate with her boyfriend.

We had changed onto another tram and passed a couple of stations, when rooster-feathered gendarmes boarded the tram. The rooster-feathered gendarmes were the policemen of the provincial towns. Now they were also the helping hands of the Arrow Cross, the Hungarian Nazis. Everyone wearing a yellow star had to get off the tram. They took us to a small police station on the outskirts of the town. There were many others already there, young and old, parents, children, babies, all taken from the trams and the streets of Budapest.

We didn't know why we were there or what was in store for us. It was late evening when we were told that we would have to spend the night in the yard and that they would take us further the next day. Kati and I lay down next to each other in the grass, but we couldn't fall asleep. It was very cold, we were wearing light summer dresses, and children were crying. I moved away a short distance because I couldn't bear the crying, and I dozed off. A gendarme lay down next to me and tried to tear my clothes off. I fought him with all my might. To subdue me he put his rifle butt under my chin. I was choking and shaking with fright when a miracle happened—air raid sirens sounded, followed immediately by bombs dropping from airplanes. The gendarme jumped up, terrified.

We were herded into the building to make sure that nobody escaped. I looked at my watch—it was midnight exactly. This was the first of many midnight raids by the Allies. When the sirens wailed again to signal that the raid was over, the gendarmes herded us back out to the yard.

This time I made sure to lie down near the crying chil-

There were many others already there

dren in case the gendarme who had attacked me returned. He did come back looking for me, but he didn't see me. He found my friend Kati instead. At first Kati tried to resist him. Then she tried to bargain with him. She told him that he could do anything he wanted with her if he let her go in the morning. He promised, and it got quieter. There were many awake that night in addition to me who were full witnesses to what happened.

The next day the gendarmes made us board the trams again. Kati sat next to the door, expecting her gendarme to let her go. Instead, he screamed at her coarsely to go sit with the others. The whole trip she begged him with her eyes, but he ignored her.

After a long journey we arrived at the Ludovika garrison, which was the Hungarian equivalent of West Point. There were as many of us as stars in the sky. We found out that the rooster-feathered gendarmes had occupied the city in very large numbers and had rounded up all the Jews they could find on the trams and streets of Budapest. We stood in lines all day in the courtyard and listened to gendarme officers harangue us. They said that Jews were a danger to the country so they had to separate us from the Hungarian people. At the same time, they were bringing in more people.

I was suffering from hunger and especially from thirst. We had been standing for hours in the hot sun. I offered a guard standing next to me my wristwatch for a little bread and water. He took it and asked also for the necklace that I had received from Erno Hollander. I gave it to him. He left and never returned.

Not far from us a well-dressed blonde woman, about thirty years old, suddenly spoke up. She said she was an American citizen visiting Budapest and they should let her go. She took out her passport to prove the truth of what she was saying. An officer with a whip in his hand led her away. Pretty soon we heard blood-curdling screams and the sound of whipping. She kept repeating that she was an American citizen, and he would reply, "This is for you, American citizen." Then we heard the sound of the whip followed by her scream. This went on until she got too exhausted and too hurt to scream. Then they threw her back to us. Her face was black and blue, bloody, and smeared with her lipstick. Her body was limp as a rag. We watched her, frozen with fear. We couldn't believe such things could be happening. A feeling of something terrible about to happen overwhelmed us.

From the Ludovika barracks the gendarmes made us walk to the brick factory at Bekasmegyer. It was a sunny day but the sun didn't shine for us. We marched in an endless column, five abreast, with young children and old people who, exhausted from the previous night, could barely move. This turned into the longest day of my life. We had walked the whole day with no food, no water, no stops to relieve ourselves. There is no more effective way to peel off a person's self-respect than to force him to march when he needs to relieve himself, and then force him to march after he has soiled himself. It was dark when we arrived at Bekasmegyer, thoroughly exhausted and demoralized. There even more people were crowded together under horrible circumstances. There was no food, no shelter, no bathrooms.

The authorities in charge had chosen the brick factory because a railroad ran through it to facilitate shipment of bricks. Thousands of people a day were being sent to Germany in cattle cars—to work, according to the guards. Between eighty and one hundred were packed into each car.

We were supposed to board in the order of arrival, but when a freight train arrived, some people tried to get on before their turn because they wanted to get away. They thought there could be nothing worse in store for them.

I thought it best not to say anything to Kati about what had happened to her, but she still felt uncomfortable around me, and avoided me. I sat next to a young woman who had a baby and a two-year-old child with her. She must have been picked up from her home because she came prepared. She had food for the babies and blankets for them to sit on. I tried to help her take care of the children. Grateful, she gave

Eighty to one hundred in a cattle car

me a little food. She also had a needle and thread with her and I was able to repair my dress a little. When she saw that I was freezing at night she gave me one of her children's blankets. I watched the children for her when she went to get some water or to use the latrine. The latrine was a long ditch under the open sky with a beam laid along its top. Everybody sat down on the beam, next to each other. It was humiliating.

We had been at the brick factory for a few days when, one night, someone stole the children's food. I was so angry I cried along with the mother. I couldn't let it be, so I asked one of the guards to try to find the food. He did—a boy of about twelve had stolen it. He too was just a hungry, terrified child. In punishment the guard, standing over him and pointing a rifle at the boy's head, made him do fifty push-ups while we waited for our turn on the freight trains leaving for Germany.

I Escape

In the meantime, the Stolyai government fell and was followed by the Lakatos government. The Stolyai government must have overreached itself in its zealous persecution of Jews even by current standards of public opinion, for when the Lakatos government came into power, it was announced over loudspeakers that those who were picked up from the trams or the streets could go home to fetch blankets and a change of clothes, as long as they returned the same day. Kati and I immediately presented ourselves to return home. There were many others. We were all taken back to the city on trams, in groups of ten, accompanied by a guard. On the way there I whispered to Kati that if we did not tell them our correct address, perhaps we could escape. The guard, with a list of names in his hand, dropped everybody off at his or her house. He told us that he was going out for lunch and that afterwards he would come and pick up each of us. He dropped off two girls at 69 Nep Szinhaz Street, a very large starred building in which my sister was living. I said I lived there, too. I had lost the heel of one shoe and could barely walk, but I ran up to the fifth floor to Fajgi's room. I told her what had happened to me and that I had decided not to go back.

When the guard came back he called out names from the courtyard. I saw a girl with a package descend from the fourth floor and another girl with a package, descend from the second floor. The guard kept calling my name. Then he went to the superintendent to find out where exactly Rozsi Katz lived. There were hundreds of people living in the building and it was the superintendent's job to know exactly where everybody was. I am sure she told him, in no uncertain terms, that no one by that name lived in the building.

I was hiding by the door waiting to see what would happen next. In the apartment my sister and the people she was sharing the apartment with were all trembling. I tried to reassure them by telling them that I didn't tell anybody where I was going, but I was shaking, too. Finally, cursing, the guard gave up and left. I took a shower, got some clean clothes and shoes from Fajgi and felt like a human being again.

I did not sew the yellow star back on my clothes. I was determined to avoid any road that might lead back to the brick factory in Bekasmegyer. But I could be arrested for disobeying the law that said that Jews were supposed to wear a yellow star. Not having identification papers was even more severely punished. What I needed was a false ID. Through the Union I had known some girls from Slovakia who had obtained them, and I wished now that I had paid closer attention when they were talking about it. It took money and connections to buy identification papers. I had very little money and I didn't know whom to turn to. My only hope was to find some of the people I knew from the union. One by one, I went to the places where we used to hang out. There was no more direct way of contacting anyone. The union had been shut down for some time by then.

It was a beautiful sunny day, with a high blue sky, full of soft white clouds. The store display windows sparkled in the sunshine. Dressed in a brightly colored cotton dress I went from place to place wrestling with my worries. There wasn't much of a chance that I would run into someone I knew. Still, it was the only chance I had. It was risky to be out on the streets without identification papers. Still, it was no worse than having papers which identified me as Jewish. Suddenly I heard a commotion ahead of me. A police raid! They were becoming daily routines. Policemen in uniforms and armed civilians with Arrow Cross armbands were stopping everybody on the street, checking their papers. I entered the nearest building. One of two large entry doors was open. In the courtyard to my right, a narrow sign read, "Building Superintendent." I knocked on the door. "It's open," a voice from inside answered. I entered. A middle-aged woman, dressed in a dark blue cotton dress with small white dots was sitting on a fancy divan in the kitchen. She held a gold-rimmed saucer in one hand, and sipped coffee from a fine matching cup she held awkwardly in her other hand. I could tell that both the cup and the divan were recent acquisitions, and that she had not bought them from her superintendent's salary.

"Good morning," I said. "I am looking for a two-bedroom apartment for my parents." I looked around and was startled by the quantity of expensive furnishings crammed into the kitchen. There was a Persian rug on the wall behind the divan; above the rug, a picture in a golden frame much too ornate for a photograph of a much decorated gendarme sergeant with a big handlebar mustache; through the glass door of the kitchen cabinet, the rest of the gold-rimmed china set; on the kitchen table, next to another steaming cup of coffee, a beautiful large crystal vase filled with ugly artificial flowers. The incongruity of a superintendent giving herself lady-like airs while surrounded by so much stolen stuff was ludicrous.

"Sit down, young lady," the woman said, pointing to a plush chair next to the table in the middle of the room.

"Thank you," I said, but I sat next to her on the divan. "My parents want to move from Szolnok…"

"Who is that, Mom?" interrupted a voice from the other room.

Through the open door I could see part of the bedroom—two beds with towering pillows and quilts, part of a sofa, a dresser with an oval mirror.

"It's a young girl looking for an apartment," the woman answered. "Come on, Helen. Drink your coffee. It's getting cold."

"I'll be there in a minute, Mom," the voice from the other room called. Then it sang, "I hate the wild flower-covered fields" along with Katalin Karadi on the radio.

The older woman smiled indulgently, pleased to have me as an audience for this enchanting idyll. "Would you like a cup of coffee?" she asked.

"Thank you. It smells so good. Is it real coffee?" I asked politely.

"No. No. It's just chicory and some roasted barley. With the war you know...." She smiled, put her coffee on the cabinet and brought me a cup of coffee in a lovely gold-rimmed cup and saucer.

I made room for her to sit down next to me, and went on chattering. "My father, you know, works for the Szolnok Commercial Bank. He has been doing the inventory of Jewish goods abandoned by the Jews when they were taken away. There is so much work, even my mom had to help. She didn't even get paid for it. But now the Russian front is getting so close to Szolnok, we think it would be best for them to move here to Budapest." I was signaling with everything in my power that we were her kind of people. But now it was time for her to say something. Luckily, I noticed among the knickknacks on the cabinet the picture of a young soldier with a nicely trimmed mustache. A narrow black ribbon with a bow in the center was tied around the lower part of the frame. I let my eyes linger tellingly on the picture.

"It's her husband," the old woman said, nodding with her head towards the bedroom. "He died in February on the Russian front. He ran over a field mine with his truck. He was a mechanic. He was going to open his own bicycle repair shop after the war."

I made sympathetic noises. I figured that by now, the raid outside must be very close. I had to stay in the apartment as long as possible. I took another sip of the coffee, wiped a non-existent tear from my eye, and said in a low, sad voice:

"My fiancé was also killed on the Eastern front. About a year ago. He also died a hero's death. His patrol was ambushed."

She put an arm on my shoulder and said in a voice full with sympathy, "This war has demanded great sacrifices from the Magyar people." Then her voice became suffused with hatred. "All this because of the international Jewish and Communist conspiracy. But don't you worry, my girl. The war will be over soon with our final victory. The Germans have a new secret weapon."

The conversation was taking a promising turn. It should take at least five minutes to get through talking about secret weapons. Helen joined us, holding a baby tied with ribbons to a big pillow. In her late twenties, she was a blonde with light blue eyes, deep red lipstick, and heavy makeup. A silver necklace with a cross hung over the white lace collar of her black, silk-like dress. She laid the baby on the divan next to me, took the cup of coffee from the table, and sat down in a chair facing us. Three well-dressed women, sipping coffee, looking at the baby, we presented a cozy picture when a second later the door opened with a loud bang. Two men with Arrow Cross armbands and shotguns in their hands were standing in the doorway. One was in his late forties, the other in his late teens.

"Where is the superintendent?" asked the older one in a rough voice.

"I am the superintendent," the old woman said, standing up. "What is the problem?"

My heart was pounding in my chest, but I managed to look calm and uninterested.

"Are there any Jews in the building?" the older man asked.

"No, thank God. They were all taken away last week," the woman answered.

"Are you sure?" the men asked, in somewhat softer voices, seeing the picture on the wall.

"Of course I am sure. It's my job to keep the register of

all the tenants," she answered with indignation.

"Let's go, we have work to do," said the older Arrow Cross man as he saw his younger partner eyeing me with interest. They left, closing the door.

"They are overworked," said the woman, as she sat down. "These Jews are such a problem."

I nodded approvingly. I needed to stay a little longer to make sure that the raid had moved away. I put my hand on the baby's pillow.

"How old is she?" I asked, smiling at Helen.

"It's a boy. He is almost seven months old," she answered proudly.

"He looks like his grandpa," I said, pointing to the picture above.

"Yes," said the grandma with a giggle. "Only he doesn't have a mustache yet. If only he had lived to see those Christ-killers taken away. He died five years ago of liver poisoning."

There was more about dirty Jews and Christ-killers who were poisoning the decent, hard-working Magyars, and I had to sit through it because I didn't want to arouse her suspicion. Finally, at a lull during her tirade of hate, I looked at the clock on the wall and jumped up. "Oh, we got carried away," I exclaimed. "Do you have a two-bedroom apartment?"

"Oh, yes, we have more than one," they both assured me. We have all those apartments vacated by the Jews. Tell your parents to come here. We would like to have a nice Christian family like yours live here."

I hugged the old woman, shook hands with Helen, petted the baby, and left. Once outside, I took a deep breath. I was shaking inside. It was dismaying to come face-to-face with someone so steeped in official Nazi propaganda. It was hard to allow so much irrational hatred to wash over me without flinching. But it also made me more determined than ever. I told myself, "I will not give in! They will not get me!"

Christian ID

I went to my workplace and I told Mr. Klemencsics and Maria Kirtag what had happened to me. Maria, who had been doing my work in my absence, asked me if there was anything she could do to help me. I remembered that she frequently talked of her younger sister Ilona, who was studying drama in Germany. I asked her to bring me a copy of her sister's birth certificate. If I pretended I was Ilona Kirtag I could obtain a genuine residency permit and would have nothing to worry about. Maria agreed.

Mr. Klemencsics said I shouldn't stay at work where everybody knew I was Jewish. It was safer if I started afresh with my new identity. He gave me fifty pengos, which was a respectable sum of money, and he told me that if I ever needed money I shouldn't hesitate to come to him.

That same day Maria left for her hometown to get her sister's birth certificate from the town hall. While I waited for her in her apartment, I wrote to Erno Hollander and to Laci Vamos. I told them not to write to me until I wrote to them with a new address. Trusting that they knew my handwriting, I signed the letter with my new name and I used Maria's address as the return address.

The next day, Maria gave me the birth certificate. I kissed and hugged her and told her I would always be grateful. She said it was only natural to try to help a person fighting for her life. I stopped worrying. I was going to have strictly kosher ID papers showing I was Christian. There would be no problem with reporting to the police precinct once I had an address.

Exempted Jews

From Maria's house I went to see Mrs. Burgheimer. She and her family were special exempted Jews because her husband had been a decorated officer who gave his life for Hungary during the First World War. They were still living at their old apartment. I told her what had happened to me, and I asked if she could find me a job as a maid or a nanny among her acquaintances. She sent me to the house of another exempted Jewish family, that of Bela Levai, a famous architect.

The Levais lived at 51 Wilmos Csaszar Street in an apartment-office combination suite that filled the whole fifth floor. I told them that I was Jewish, but had Christian papers, and that I needed food and a place to stay. They hired me right away as a live-in maid. The Levai family consisted of Mr. and Mrs. Levai; a younger brother of Mrs. Levai; a son, eighteen; a daughter; the daughter's husband, who was a physician; and their child. Mr. Levai was still allowed to work, and he had a very distinguished clientele.

Under the Lakatos government, there was an amelioration in the situation of the Jews at first. We heard on the BBC that the International Red Cross protested to Miklos Horthy, the lifetime governor of Hungary, the deportation of the Jews. For a while, the deportations from Bekasmegyer were stopped. But the new policies didn't last long.

In August, we heard on the BBC that the Romanians had joined forces with the approaching Russians to fight the Germans. The next day the Germans staged a big parade with troops, armored cars, tanks, and SS units. They were showing any Hungarians who had a mind to change sides that the Germans had a strong presence in Hungary. Budapest was bombarded daily by British airplanes. To strike back, the Hungarian Nazis and the Germans in Hungary concentrated single-mindedly on routing out and sending to their death anyone who was Jewish. New laws were passed making life more miserable for those they didn't have in their clutches yet. For example, Jews could only be on the streets between two and five in the afternoon. By two in the afternoon, there usually wasn't any bread left even for those who had ration tickets.

I was able to get bread from Szruli without ration cards. I took bread to Fajgi, Margit, Mrs. Burgheimer, Mrs. Vamos, and Duci. Mrs. Vamos and Duci, who had hoped to get through the war as condominium owners, were forced to move into a starred house at 12 Kiraly Street. I went there often. They barely knew what to do with me, so grateful were they when they saw me arrive with a loaf of bread in my bag. Mrs. Burgheimer often hugged and kissed me with tears in her eyes. The Levais knew what my errands were about and they never complained about my coming and going. They treated me like a family member.

One day as I was walking on Nep Szinhaz Street towards Teleki Plaza, taking bread to Fajgi, I met a long procession of people being herded by gendarmes down the middle of the street. Grandparents, parents, and children were walking, carrying their few belongings in bundles and suitcases. Some people had an infant in one arm and a suitcase in the other. On the sidewalk, people were going their way, oblivious to the misery unfolding before their eyes. Nobody paid attention to what happened to the Jews.

Then from another direction an open truck approached that was filled with people the Arrow Cross had just picked up from the streets. From the truck, someone called to me, "Rozsi, Rozsi, tell my parents they took me!" It was a friend, a girl named Margit. I felt people looking to see whom she was calling. Afraid that the gendarmes might pick me up too, I turned and looked around also. After all, I wasn't Rozsi Katz anymore. I was Ilona Kirtag.

That night, Mr. Levai reported at dinner that Count Eszterhazi, who was one of their clients, had come to the office to warn him that the status of exempted Jews was not going to protect them much longer and that they should try to disappear.

Papers for Fajgi

One day Mr. Wagner, the Levais' longtime accountant, asked me if I could find him a maid, a capable girl like myself. Originally from Germany, he had a little child and his wife needed help. I told him I knew somebody who was even more capable than I, but it would take at least a week to get in touch with her. I was thinking of my sister Fajgi, hoping that somehow, within a week, I'd be able to get papers for her.

For days, after I finished my work I roamed the main streets, looking for someone who might be able to help. I was lucky. One day, I met Blackie, one of my old union friends. We called him Blackie because his skin was very dark. An iron worker, he had lost the three middle fingers on his right hand in an accident. He wasn't Jewish but he was aware of what was happening to Jews. He was very glad to see me. I asked him about our common friends. After the dissolution of the union I had lost touch with most of them. He didn't have any good news. Many were in jail, arrested while distributing leaflets. Even the leader of the union, Arpad Szakasics, had been arrested.

I told him that I had Christian papers as Ilona Kirtag and asked him if he could help me obtain papers for my sister and my brother. Blackie said that he knew someone who could forge papers for me. I told him that for my twenty-year-old sister, it didn't matter what name was used, but for my sixteen-year-old brother, I wanted to use the name Tibor Kirtag—Kirtag because I wanted to be able to keep in touch with him and take care of him and Tibor because that was Szruli's Hungarian name. I told him that in my brother's case, it wasn't urgent because, not living in a starred house and working at night, he would be all right for a few more days. But my sister needed papers immediately.

We agreed to meet the next day, and he promised to bring papers for my sister. I didn't want to tell him where I lived. I trusted him and he had always liked me, but he wasn't Jewish and one never knew. There was no point in taking unnecessary chances. The next night, at the appointed time, he was there with the papers for Fajgi. It was a miracle. I thought God must have sent him to me. At first he wouldn't take the money I offered, but knowing the papers had cost him money, I insisted. Finally he accepted. We agreed to meet again in a week for papers for Szruli. I needed some time to raise more money.

Too Late to Save Fajgi

It was pouring rain the next morning when I went to Fajgi's house with the papers. When the tram turned onto Nep Szinhaz Street, my blood froze. The gendarmes were out in force. Screaming, they were forcing Jewish people out of their apartments, lining them up in groups, and marching them away. Wails and screams filled the air. Many houses had big posters announcing, "From this house, we have smoked out all the Jews." I was silently praying, "Please, God, don't let them get to Fajgi's house before I do. Please, God, I have papers and a job waiting for her. She can be saved! Please, God, give me just a few more minutes." I thought it safer to stay on the tram until it passed her house instead of getting off at the usual stop. When the tram passed her house the sky fell on me. Her house too had a poster on its entrance proclaiming, "From this house we have smoked out all Jews."

I stayed on the tram for a few more stations to see where the endless procession of misery was going. With their hands raised, people were being marched in the rain toward the

Eastern Train Station. Then I knew their destination was the Taterzal Horse Racing Track, next to the train station. During the last few days, cattle trains had taken thousands away from there. Although the train station had recently been bombed and the trains had stopped, the gendarmes continued crowding more people into the track grounds.

Changing trams, I went home. It was a short walk from the tram station to the Levais' but I was wet to the skin before I got home. My sister and thousands of others were marching in the rain with their hands held above their heads.

A big pile of unwashed dishes was waiting for me. Crying, I did the dishes and told the Levais how I had obtained papers for my sister but was too late to save her. They felt very sorry for me but there was nothing they or anyone else could do.

Swedish Passes and Wallenberg

The Levais found out that the Swedish Embassy was issuing Shutz passes, letters declaring that the bearer was under the protection of the Swedish embassy. The Hungarian officials honored these passes even though the Swedish Embassy had no power to enforce them. The Levais dressed me up in a very expensive fur coat and hat and they sent me to the Swedish Embassy on Vadasz Street to obtain passes. I looked so impressive I could hardly recognize myself.

In front of the embassy, there were a thousand people standing in line. Not wearing a yellow star, I walked by the guards confidently, like someone who belonged there. They let me pass without a word. Once inside the office I gave my long list to a clerk.

There were many people in the room and the phones kept ringing. I saw a tall man run out of an inner office and hurriedly stuff papers into his briefcase. He said he was on his way to Soprony to stop a train. Then a secretary ran over with more passes, and called him "Mr. Wallenberg." I had seen the famous Raoul Wallenberg.

Raoul Wallenberg was a young Swedish diplomat who had come to Budapest in 1944. He defied top German Nazis such as Adolph Eichman as well as the Hungarian Nazi Arrow Cross, saving as many Jews as he could. He tried to establish protected houses, and declared all Jews living inside them Swedish citizens. He would show up at sites destroyed by bombs which were being cleared by labor service units, and he would issue everyone in the unit Swedish passports, or, when he ran out of those, handwritten papers which said that the bearer was entitled to Swedish passports. Somtimes he stopped trains, issuing papers to everybody on the train. He was last seen in 1945, during the last few days of the war, within the Russian army zone of occupation. He was being led away by Russian officers. He has never been seen again. He is credited with having saved between 30,000 and 100,000 Hungarian Jews. The State of Israel decreed that Wallenberg was a Righteous Gentile.

Rumors persisted for many years that he was still alive, buried somewhere in the Russian Gulag. Simon Wiesenthal, who believed that Wallenberg deserved the Nobel Peace Prize, valiantly tried to find him in the Soviet Union, but he met with no success. Many believe that, in spite of repeated claims to have no knowledge of him, the Soviet Union had intentionally covered up his whereabouts to avoid international embarassment.

I carried home protective passes for everybody in the extended Levai family. I had brought them safety for a few more days. In gratitude, one of the sisters-in-law handed me a hundred pengo bill.

I Buy Fajgi's Life with the Last of Mamma's Necklace

Three days later I learned that people were being sent home from the Taterzal Race Track to get blankets and warm clothes. I rushed immediately to the building where my sister lived, but the entrance was locked. I tried to convince the superintendent that I needed to deliver an urgent message to someone, but she said it was out of the question. She had received strict orders that nobody was allowed to come in or go out. I stood in front of the gate helpless, unable to think of any plan. It was getting dark when, through the entrance window, I saw the assistant superintendent with a mop and a broom in hand. She was a friendly looking young woman. I knocked on the window and she opened the door. I told her that I had a very urgent message for Fani Katz, who lived on the fifth floor, and if she would bring Fani down, I would pay her well for her trouble. She agreed. When she brought Fajgi down, I told her that I would give her a thick gold necklace, if she let Fajgi out. She said she wouldn't dare. I told her nobody would find out, forced into her hand what was left of Mamma's necklace, and didn't wait for her reply. I opened the door, shoved Fajgi out, and we walked away while the assistant superintendent was still busy explaining how she was afraid to let Fajgi go.

I tore off Fajgi's yellow star and we ran for the tram. It all happened so quickly that my sister barely knew what world she was in. She was frightened and exhausted. Having returned home in the small hours of the night after days of standing in the rain, she was barely able to move. On the tram, she pulled herself in to make herself small and she hung her head. The tram was full of people and we were standing very close to each other. Whispering, I ordered her to stand up straight and keep her head high. She looked at me with eyes full of tears, but she listened. We were lucky.

We made it to the Levais' house without incident.

It was after dinner when we arrived. The Levais shared in my joy at rescuing my sister. I quickly cleared the table and sat Fajgi down to eat. Then while we washed the dishes, Fajgi described what she'd been through. It was pretty much as I had imagined. They had stood in the rain, crowded together, for three days and three nights. There were thousands of people and there weren't even any restrooms for them.

I told her of the job waiting for her and gave her the Christian papers. According to the papers, she was Ibolya Tomojoga, an illiterate from Jozsefhaza. I also told her of our brother's new identity. When we went to sleep Fajgi started saying the Krishme—the Hebrew prayer one says before bed. I told her to forget it and learn the Lord's Prayer instead. It was a prayer all Christians knew and the Nazis asked girls to recite it if they suspected them of being Jewish. Males they identified by pulling their pants down.

When Mr. Wagner came to work the next morning, I told him my girlfriend had arrived and was ready to start her job as a maid. He was very happy and gave me a tip of twenty pengos. When he went home that night he took Fajgi with him. I was relieved. Fajgi was safe.

For a while we used to meet on Sunday afternoons. She slept in the kitchen on a folding bed which she put away during the day. She cooked, cleaned, and took care of the baby. Mrs. Wagner, who was much younger than her husband, liked to sleep in, and spent a lot of time socializing with her friends. One morning, Fajgi was changing the baby in the bedroom and Mrs. Wagner was combing her hair in front of the dresser mirror when the bell rang. Mrs. Wagner motioned to my sister to finish changing the baby and she answered the door. Through the open door Fajgi could see in the entry doorway a young woman with a yellow star on her coat, shifting her weight from one leg to another, upset and embarrassed. Fajgi couldn't hear what they said, but she found out later that day at lunch, the main meal of the day. Mrs. Wagner said, "You know what happened this morning? Remember those Jews who used to live on the second floor? Grun something? The woman came by this morning asking if we would let her have her baby's bed? Her child cries and can't sleep at night because he misses his bed. Imagine the nerve. Where shall I put my baby? I told her that she won't need the bed much longer anyhow. They will all be taken to Germany." Mr. Wagner, who had come for lunch, didn't say anything.

Death Marches

In the middle of October there were rumors that the governor, Miklos Horthy, was going to make a proclamation. We were anticipating it eagerly, thinking it might mean good news. On the radio, Horthy announced that Hungary would no longer fight alongside the Germans against Allied troops. He spoke for more than an hour. The upshot of it all was that he was taking Hungary out of the war. We were euphoric. But our joy didn't last long. Early in the afternoon on the same day, the arrest of Horthy was broadcast on the radio. The next morning it was announced that Parliament had formed a new government from the Arrow Cross Party under the direction of Szalasi. The news bombarded us from public loud speakers. Szalasi declared himself leader of the nation.

What it really meant was that the relentless war against the Jews was further intensified. Under Szalasi, the Arrow Cross Party and the Germans took over the supervision of the destruction of the Hungarian Jews. They formed a ghetto in Budapest. All Jews from the starred houses and all exempted Jews had to move into the ghetto. From there they sent tens of thousands of people on death marches to Germany. The train tracks having been bombed, people were

Death march

made to walk to Hegyes Halom and from there to Germany. Thousands died on the road.

In the meantime, Budapest was bombarded daily by the Allies. Once when the Levais and I took refuge in a bomb shelter, one of the tenants started shouting, "For how long do we have to breathe the same air as these dirty Jews!" Mr. Levai just looked at him without uttering a word. His ten-year-old granddaughter hid behind her mother's back, terrified. Nobody else said anything. After that the Levais didn't go down to the bomb shelter no matter how heavy the bombardment.

On the night of Horthy's speech, I stayed up late to be sure to meet my brother at the bakery. I wanted to give him his Christian identification papers, which I had obtained in the meantime, and I wanted to discuss the news with him. I did not find him there and was told that he hadn't been to work for days. Worried, I went to his apartment. Since it was not in a starred house, I had no trouble getting in, but he was not home. I went back again in the evening. This time the gate was closed and I was afraid to ring the superintendent. If Szruli was in trouble, I would get into trouble by looking for him. I walked up and down the street in front of the house, waiting to go in with someone who lived there. It was late at night by the time someone finally showed up. I said hello to him and struck up a conversation. I told him how lucky it was for me to have gotten there at the same time as he.

"This way I won't have to bother the superintendent," I said.

He asked me whose apartment I was going to.

"A young man," I told him, smiling.

"Your young man has good taste," he replied, and he let me in.

Waiting until he was out of sight so he wouldn't know where I was headed, I ran to my brother's second-floor apartment and knocked on the door. Miraculously, he was there. But his appearance scared me.

Captured while walking on the street, he had been marched outside the city with a large group of people. Those who could not keep up with the pace of the march were lined up next to the ditch on the side of the road and shot. This happened more than once, and many people died that way. Szruli decided that whatever the destination might have been, nothing good awaited him there. So towards the evening of the second day, as the guards were executing people, he pretended to fall dead, rolling into the ditch at the side of the road. He stayed there in the mud and the rain until everybody was gone. Then it had taken him a couple of days to make it home undetected. He had just gotten home when I arrived. He had not even had time to clean up.

I gave him his Christian papers and told him the next day we would get him an apartment closer to the bakery and to me so that he would have to spend less time on the street. I rented him a bed in the ground floor apartment of the assistant superintendent in the building the Levais lived in. It was just across the street from the bakery where he worked. With both of us in the same building, it would be easier for us to stay in touch with each other.

The next day, we walked to the police precinct to report my brother's address under his new identity as Tibor Kirtag. We were on the Korut, a circular avenue in the heart of the city, when a young punk with a big rifle on his shoulders stopped us. He must have smelled the ordeal Szruel had just been through, because, pointing his rifle at Szruel, he said, "You are Jewish, I can see it on your face!"

"You are Jewish!"

I thought, "What on earth do I do now?" Then I thought, "I am not going to let this little punk take my brother from me."

Aloud, in a voice of great superiority, I said, "Of course he is Jewish! But he is mine. I am taking him to the district office of the Arrow Cross. They'll take care of him there." I pushed my brother along by the shoulder and added roughly, "Get going!" We went on. We made it to the police station and we got permission for him to stay at his new address.

Margit and the Levais Go into Hiding

I stopped at Margit's house to see if she needed false identification papers and to tell her what had happened to us. I wanted to help her avoid being forced into the ghetto. She said she didn't need my help. She had obtained papers, and she and Eva were about to move to the suburbs. They had found a room in a house with a garden. Eva would be able to go to school. I took her new address and left.

When I got home I found that the Levais' eighteen-year-old son and Mrs. Levai's seventeen-year-old brother had received orders to present themselves immediately for labor service. Andrew, their son, was assigned to a company which was housed near the Western Train Station in a big old warehouse. Early each morning they were taken to the outskirts of the city to dig trenches and tank traps against the approaching Soviet troops. The family sent me there with new ID papers to help him escape. I went to the station, but I couldn't find him among the hundreds of young men who were being marched to work, guarded by armed soldiers. As I walked along the column looking for him, I asked many to spread the word that I'd be back when they returned from work, and he should try to march at the outer edge of the column so that I could find him. I did find him in the evening. Walking alongside the column I told him that I had new papers. I told him to take my arm and walk away with me, pretending that we didn't belong there. He looked at me frightened and said, "I can't. Look at me. I am tired and dirty. They'll recognize me at once. We'll both be shot."

As we were talking, a guard saw me. He rushed over yelling, "What do you want from that Jew boy? Aren't you ashamed of yourself? Can't you find yourself a decent Christian boy of your own kind?" The window of opportunity had closed. I ran away. Back home I had to face his parents with the news I was not able to bring him home. He had been afraid to take a chance. He didn't come back.

Early next morning I opened the door to the urgent ringing of Count Eszterhazi. He came to the apartment, not the office, and told the Levais to disappear immediately. Everyone moved that very day. Mr. and Mrs. Levai fled to a one-room apartment in a cellar in Zugliget, their daughter and granddaughter to a rented room in another part of the town. Their son-in-law, a physician, arranged to be admitted to the hospital for a chronic illness under a false name. I don't know for sure but I think it was Count Eszterhazi who obtained Christian papers for everyone. A very humane person, he was a Hungarian patriot and strongly anti-Nazi. Unfortunately, there were few Hungarians like him.

Now I was alone in the Levais' apartment. Before leaving, they had shown me their store of canned food, which was kept in the office on shelves under the drafting tables, and they asked me to bring it to them little by little. I started a routine of delivering food to each of them every day.

Because I didn't like being alone, I spent most of my time with a girl the same age as I who lived with her mother on the second floor. Her father was on the Russian front and we used to listen together to the BBC for news. They didn't know I was Jewish. Like everyone else in the house, they thought I was a Hungarian Christian who, having fled the advancing Russians, was renting a room from the Levais.

Eva Walks to Bergen-Belsen

A few days later, I left for Margit's new address, carrying a loaf of bread, a few cans of food, an egg, and some sugar cubes. Anticipating how happy little Eva would be when I gave her the sugar, I silently thanked God that at least a few of us were still safe. When I arrived, the owner told me they no longer lived there. Shortly after they moved in, as Margit was taking Eva to the first day of school, they were met in the doorway by the Arrow Cross, who took them away. I tried to keep my face blank and left quickly. I found out later that they were denounced by the person who had sold them the false identification papers.

Margit and little Eva were made to walk in the cold rain and mud. Dressed up to take Eva to school on the first day, Margit was wearing heels. Not able to keep up, she was told to stay behind for the wagon for those who could not walk. There was no wagon. Margit was shot on the side of the road to Hegyes Halom along with thousands of others who could not keep up. Eva marched on, holding the hand of a woman who had a slightly older daughter.

They walked for many days to Bergen-Belsen. Sitting on the bed in the barracks, Eva watched the door, waiting for her mother to walk in. Finally, Eva was told to lie down and go to sleep. Then she started to cry. She was afraid to lie down next to her bunk mate. The lady was very cold and she was afraid that if she laid down next to her, she too would get cold like that. She had started to school and ended up a few days later in Bergen-Belsen, in the same bunk with a corpse.

The inmates of the camp were starving. One day a pile of potato peels was left in the cellar under the kitchen. Eva, who was small enough to fit though the window, was sent to bring out the peels. Once in, however, she sat on top of the pile and started eating. The others kept signaling to her, asking her to bring some for them, but Eva couldn't stop herself. Only after she had her fill did she carry the peels out for the others.

At the end of the war, sick with typhus and infested with lice, the Red Cross took Eva to Sweden. She lived there for three years until somebody recognized her. She returned to Hungary when she was ten years old.

On the Run

I could still get bread from Szruli. So I kept up my routine of visiting the few people I could reach. On the streets some houses had signs saying that the tenants were under the protection of foreign embassies. But the Arrow Cross had started forcing people out of the protected houses. At the same time, the Germans were dynamiting the bridges in Budapest without warning to the civilian population. Many people died in the explosions. The railroads had been bombed, but still the SS, the Arrow Cross, and the gendarmes thought it their most important task to round up as many Jews as possible and march them to their deaths.

I spent most of my time with my new friend on the second floor of the building because it wasn't prudent to be on the street and I didn't like being alone. One early afternoon, my coat on over my shoulder, I started down the stairs toward her apartment. On the third-floor landing I met four armed Arrow Cross goons. I greeted them, smiling. They asked me where Ilona Kirtag lived. I answered them without hesitation, "On the fifth floor." They continued up, and I, forcing myself to walk slowly, went out the gate.

If Ilona Kirtag was sought by the Hungarian Nazis, Tibor Kirtag was not safe either and I needed to warn him. I found my brother at the bakery.

"What should I do? Where should I go?" he asked me. I told him I didn't know. I didn't know yet where I was going to sleep that night. I only knew that he should not go home under any circumstances. "Better sleep in the storage room on top of the flour sacks," I told him.

Once again I asked Mrs. Burgheimer for help. She gave me the address of some old friends of hers who she thought might need a maid and she told me to use her as a reference. I went right away to the address she had given me. It was in Buda, at 7 Hatyu Street. The people were an older couple, the man a retired engineer. They had a big, beautiful villa. I told them my story: Mrs. Burgheimer had sent me; I was escaping from the advancing Russians; I needed food and a place to stay; I wanted to work for them. The lady of the house asked me what I could do. I told her truthfully that I didn't know how to cook but I knew how to clean and I could learn anything she wanted to teach me. She hired me on the spot.

Feeling safe again, I relaxed. Buda seemed a world away from Pest. It was a neighborhood of large villas with gardens owned by rich people. There were no starred houses, no Germans in sight, no horrors to see. Even the bombs which fell twice a day on Pest seemed to avoid Buda.

The elderly couple were happy with me. I did the grocery shopping and the cleaning. I remember waxing the floor with a big black brush under one foot and a rag under the other. I cleaned and cleaned even though everything was already quite clean. I knew that the war would soon be over. Though the radio and the newspapers were still full of stories abut the heroic victories of the Hungarian and German armies, the Russians were closing in on Budapest. I thought that I would make it. I thought often of my brother and sister. Were they still alive? I wondered how the Levais, for whom I had functioned as a lifeline, were managing. Did they think that I had abandoned them? I could no longer help anyone else. I had left with nothing but the dress I was wearing, and I could not go back.

One day my employer sent me to the butcher to buy meat for a stew. There wasn't any stew meat so I telephoned to ask what to buy instead. The woman answered the phone and asked me in a tone of exaggerated surprise, "Ilona, you are Jewish? I had no idea! The Arrow Cross is here, waiting for you." I hung up without a word and started walking. "Dear God," I thought, "what do I do now? Where do I go? How did they find me?" I tried going to Mrs. Burgheimer yet again for help but they were no longer at their house. They were set on waiting the war out in their apartment, so they must have been taken away. I don't know if they survived the war.

In despair, I went back to my former place of work to see Mr. Klemencsics and Maria. I wanted to find out why my ID, which wasn't even a forgery, no longer protected me. I went straight to the cutting room. Mr. Klemencsics, the chief tailor, and everyone else were really happy to see me. Maria was no exception. She hugged and held me, looked at me, and then hugged and held me again. I told her I needed to talk to her in private. We went to a dressing room, and I asked her what had happened, why weren't her sister's papers good anymore?

She told me her sister had come home from Germany for Christmas vacation and had stayed at Maria's apartment for a few days. While she was staying there, a letter with her name as the sender was returned as undeliverable. She opened it and saw that it was written to a boy in the labor service. It was the letter I had written to Erno Hollander. Outraged, she went to the Arrow Cross party headquarters to announce that a Jewish girl was using her name and she demanded that they do everything they could to catch her. Maria was deeply sorry. She kept repeating that there was nothing she could do and that it wasn't her fault. I told her that I was grateful for what she had already done. At least now I knew where I stood. My friend had not betrayed me.

But wherever I went in Budapest as Ilona Kirtag, the Arrow Cross would pursue me.

I asked Mr. Klemencsics to lend me some money. He gave me all the money he had in his wallet. Touched by his gesture, I started to cry. He held my arms, kissed my forehead, and said, "Watch out for yourself, my girl." I said goodbye and left. I felt helpless and hopeless. I had no idea where to go, or what to do next, and by now it was afternoon.

I walked the streets of Budapest aimlessly, trying to figure out where to go. Not watching where I was going, I finally noticed the sign "Nagyfuvaros Street." The name sounded familiar. Suddenly I remembered. Weeks ago, I heard a friend of Mrs. Levai mention it. To avoid being forced into the ghetto, she had considered taking her child to the Red Cross Orphanage on Nagyfuvaros Street. Quickening my steps, I started looking for the orphanage, first in the direction I had been walking in, then in the other direction. It was almost dusk. Very few people were on the street, and everybody was trying to get home before dark. I figured I would ask the people at the orphanage to let me stay overnight because I got caught too far away from home. I kept searching, but there was no sign of the orphanage. I was getting desperate. Finally I found it: a white oval sign with a fat red cross in the middle and, around the cross in red letters, the words "The International Swiss Red Cross Orphanage."

I rang the doorbell. No answer. I knocked on the door to the entrance hall. No answer. I pushed down the door handle. It was open. Inside the entry, two staircases led to the upper floors. There were several doors downstairs. The first led to an empty office. The second to a large dining room with long tables and benches. A strange, muffled moan came from upstairs. Following it, I found the children in a large, smelly, dark room, huddled together, trying to warm themselves with their own bodies. They were shivering and

crying softly. The same scene was repeated in the next room.
I saw a little girl holding the hand of a small boy who was
lying on the floor. When I approached, I could see that the
boy was dead. I told the little girl to let go of him. "I can't,"
she said, crying. "My mommy told me to never let go of his
hand." Now crying myself, I hugged her, gently pried open
her fingers and removed the dead child to an empty office. I
tried to comfort some of the other children. Finally, exhausted, shivering with cold, my heart heavy at the sight of
so much misery, I sat down on a chair in an empty office
overlooking the rooms and turned up my coat collar to warm
myself with my breath. The tears were still burning my eyes.
To my surprise, I fell asleep. When I opened my eyes next,
daylight was seeping in through the blackout paper covering
the windows. I looked for the kitchen and found it past the
dining room. Turning on the light switch, I saw, to my dis-
gust, hundreds of cockroaches running for cover from the
top of the big built-in stove, the shelves filled with huge pots
and pans, the large kitchen tables. The pantry was bare—
nothing but empty shelves, empty jars, empty containers.
Not a trace of food. I couldn't understand the situation. How
long since the children had eaten? Why were they alone?
Where were the adults who were supposed to take care of
them? What had happened? Heartsick and haunted by the
bluish-gray faces of the children, I left. I couldn't take care of
all of them alone. I couldn't even take care of myself. And I
couldn't face them again knowing that they were starving
and I was helpless to do something about it.

The cold had let up. Treading the melting snow under
my feet, I went back to the Korut (Circle Avenue). Cold and
hungry, I entered a busy coffee shop and ordered a hot coffee. I read a newspaper, which was on the table, then went to
the ladies' room and washed my face. I tried to stay as long
as possible without attracting attention. Eventually I had to
leave the coffee shop and continued my walk, waiting for a

miracle to happen. I was really desperate, but I knew that it must not show. By the afternoon it was cold again. An icy wind was blowing and froze the melted snow. I still didn't know where to go or what to do, or even where to stay that night. I took the tram to the end of the line. Then I got another ticket and traveled to the opposite end of the line. This attracted the attention of the conductor, so I got off and caught the next tram back to the center of the city, the Korut, got off, and walked again aimlessly.

Suddenly I felt I was being followed. I didn't look back but I could tell from the reflections in store windows that I was being followed by someone wearing the black uniform and red arm band of the Arrow Cross. I kept walking and he kept following. I was trying to force myself to comprehend what was happening, but all I could think was, "This is the end." All of a sudden he called me: "Rozsika!"

Astounded, I stopped and looked him in the face. He was an old friend of mine, Jozsi, a Jewish boy. I told him I needed a place to sleep. He said he might know of a place, but since he wasn't sure it was still there, he would escort me there. We took the tram again to the outskirts of the town. By then it was late at night. We walked to a big house but did not enter. Instead, we went to a guest house in the back of the garden. He knocked on the window and a young man answered. If he had been sleeping, he was in the habit of sleeping completely dressed.

Apparently I wasn't the first person Jozsi had taken there because the whole matter was settled in seconds. The young men let me in, he shook hands with Jozsi, and Jozsi disappeared. The guest house consisted of a small room furnished with a bed, a table, and two armchairs. I sat in an armchair and told my host that I wanted to spend the night there. He lay down on the bed, turned towards the wall, and said I could share the bed without fear of any harm. He said I could only stay a few hours because he wanted me to leave before anybody from the house woke up. I lay down next to him in my long pants and coat. I was so exhausted, I fell asleep immediately. It seemed only minutes later when he shook me awake at dawn and told me I must leave. I never found out his name and he didn't know the first thing about me. But he had helped me get through the night. It was still bitterly cold outside when I left. I had been lucky to have spent the night in a warm room. I caught the first tram and went back to the Korut.

When I arrived, a dreadful sight met my eyes. An endless column of people was being herded away under the guns of the Arrow Cross. In addition, the Arrow Cross were cheerfully hunting for people in the ruins of the bombarded houses. If a man looked suspicious, they pulled down his pants to check if he was circumcised. If he turned out to be Jewish, they shot him on the spot, or they taunted and tortured him and then threw him in with the mass of marchers. There were many corpses lying alongside the road.

The city was jam-packed with German soldiers. There were machine gun posts on the roofs of the houses in addition to anti-aircraft guns. The Russians had almost surrounded the city but the Arrow Cross, under orders from Szalasi, still thought it their first priority to round up as many Jews as possible and send them marching to their death.

Cold and at a loss for what to do next, I went into the "Hallo," an inexpensive restaurant at one end of Circle Avenue, and ordered a hot soup. From my table, I noticed an old friend, Eva, enter with another woman. I knew Eva from dance school days. A beautiful blonde girl, she also had not had to pay to go to the dance school because she attracted so many boys. Eva was overjoyed to see me. She introduced her friend, a young woman named Margo, and they joined me at my table. They were pretty much in the same position I was in. Margo's husband, accused of spying, had been arrested, and she was in hiding. Eva was Jewish and had no place to go. We were trying to decide what to do next when Margo had an idea.

She knew a news correspondent staying at the garrison in Budateteny. She thought he might be able to help us. So together, we set out on the tram for Budateteny. It was a good feeling not to be alone. After a few stations Margo decided that she had some other business to take care of first. She gave us the name of her friend, told us to use her as a reference when we found him, and got off.

As the tram approached the bridge over the Danube, we saw people lined up on the stairs to the river bank. They were surrounded by the Arrow Cross, who, in turn, were surrounded by policemen. The Arrow Cross were preparing to machine-gun the people, and the police were trying to stop them. The Budapest police were willing to cooperate with the Arrow Cross in enforcing the law and, if the law said that Jews had to be rounded up, they rounded up the Jews. But they knew of no law that said one could shoot Jews, and, to their credit, they would not allow the Arrow Cross to shoot them. This conflict between the Arrow Cross and the Budapest police occurred repeatedly. Whether people stayed alive depended on whether it was the police or the Arrow Cross who had the upper hand in the particular place and moment the conflict occurred.

We got off the tram at Budateteny late in the afternoon. In spite of our long pants, long coats, and sweaters, we were freezing. The place looked more like a village than a suburb. It was full of flower nurseries and snow-covered hot houses. We found the garrison while it was still light outside. We asked the guard to find Margo's friend. He sent a soldier to look for him. After a long time the solider returned with the news that our friend was at the front line. We asked if we could wait for him there. They laughed at us. We were back on the streets with no plan and nowhere to go.

Arrow Cross Headquarters

We started back towards the tram station. We passed a large house with a sign announcing, "Arrow Cross Party Head-quarters" and a Nazi flag at the entrance. Suddenly I had an idea. This would be the safest place for us. I persuaded Eva that we had a convincing story to tell them: we were running from the Russians; we were there because I had a brother garrisoned at the barracks; we were hoping he would know what to do next, but he wasn't there—he was fighting at the front line. Now we had to turn to our "brothers" in the Arrow Cross because we felt safe in their company and we had nowhere else to turn.

Eva thought it was too good a story not to try out, so we went in. There were only four men there, all of them older than us. Two were nondescript, one was a huge imbecilic-looking character, and their boss was a small, wide middle-aged man named Lajos Nagy. We told them our story and they believed it. They were ready to play the role of under-standing older brothers or fathers that we had suggested for them. They fed us a good dinner and entertained us with stories about how they had already sent their families ahead to a village past the Danube. Lajos Nagy said his wife and three children were already in Germany. They promised to take us with them when they decided to run away from the Russians.

In the meantime they showed us a room we could have to sleep in. They told us if we needed any clothes, we could find anything we wanted in the cellar. After dinner Eva and I cleared the table and started doing the dishes. Our hosts were getting ready to leave for Budapest. They were taking down ammunition, loading their rifles, and making other preparations. The scary giant also took a rope. We asked them where they were going and they said, "Hunting." "Jew hunting," one of them added in a completely matter-of-fact tone. Eva and I tried to avoid looking at each other.

After they left, Eva and I talked over our options. We were no longer sure that it was a good idea to stay there, but we couldn't figure out where else to go. Going to sleep was out of the question, so we were still awake when they came home.

Elated and talkative, they drank and reveled in detailed stories of the murders they'd just committed. They were gloating over the rope trick—they had tied together several people, lined them up on the bank of the Danube, and only shot one. The dead one took the others down, and they didn't have to waste any bullets. They said the water of the Danube was red from the blood. Eva and I kept silent and tried not to look at them. They were more intoxicated than the liquor they had consumed warranted. They were in ecstasy from the pleasure they were taking in the murders they had just committed.

Finally, Eva and I retired to our room. We went to bed fully dressed with long pants under our dresses. The house was quiet but we could not sleep. We kept trying to think of someplace else to go to, but decided again and again that we were safer there than on the streets.

The next day we went to the only store in the village for a bar of soap and some toothbrushes. At the store we saw large chocolate bars. Earlier, it would have never occurred to us to spend money on chocolate. Now it seemed that we were probably going to die shortly anyway, so we might as well have our fill of it. We figured that by pooling our money we could buy ten bars. We thought that it was unlikely that we would stay alive long enough to eat them, but at the same time we liked the idea of having a bar of chocolate to look forward to. So every day for the next ten days we bought a bar of chocolate.

Our hosts left on their heinous errand every evening. All four of them had started taking ropes along. We made sure not to be around when they returned so that we wouldn't have to listen to their stories. But during the day we continued to act friendly and cheerful. One night, the ugly imbecile came into our room dead drunk, intent on forcing his attentions on us. I ran crying to Lajos Nagy and woke him with, "Jani won't let us be. We ran away from the Russians to be molested by our Arrow Cross brothers!"

Lajos Nagy rushed to our room and reprimanded Jani severely, yelling "Aren't you ashamed of yourself! How would you like it if someone did this to your daughter!" He had the others carry Jani out of the room, adding for emphasis, "If this ever happens again, I will shoot you." The incident gave us an excuse to ask Lajos Nagy to find us lodgings someplace else, and he did the very next day. But we told them that we wanted to go with them when they escaped because we still had to go to their headquarters to eat. We had spent all our money on the chocolate.

Liberation

On December 20th, Lajos Nagy showed up with shovels in his hands and said everybody without exception must dig ditches to stop the advancing Russians. We went to fulfill our "patriotic" duty. For three days straight in the brutal cold, together with the rest of the population of Budateteny, we chipped away at the frozen, granite-hard earth.

On the 24th, early in the morning, Lajos Nagy showed up again to tell us that we should get ready—they were leaving at noon. I started crying and said I was tired of running and I didn't want to leave my country. I'd rather take my chances with the Russians. He said okay, but that we should still go with them so they could show us where in the cellar they had hidden the gold and jewels. There was more than they could take with them. Eva said of course we would come. She added that we had not really decided what to do yet, that she would try to convince me to go with them, and if we decided to go with them we would meet them at head-quarters in time. And she thanked him for standing by us in such trying times.

"Well," he said, "I have to go. Make up your minds!" He turned back again from the door and said, "We will be there until noon."

Eva and I couldn't believe how easy it was all turning out to be. Could they really be leaving? Could it really be over? In the afternoon we went back to the headquarters, and found they had really cleared out. First we went into the house and ate some food. There was still plenty left. Then for the first time since we were there, we went down to the cellar, which turned out to be overflowing with things they had stolen from Jewish people. We could hardly believe our eyes. There were rolls of cloth, clothes, sheets, Persian rugs, fur coats, anything movable. We pulled some clothes out for ourselves because we had only what we were wearing. We were trying to decide where the jewelry and gold might be hidden when we heard crackling and started smelling smoke. Somebody had set the house on fire. Choking from the smoke, we made our way up the stairs. We were lucky not to have been burned alive there in the cellar.

When we stepped out there were two Russian soldiers in front of us. They were wearing long coats tied around their waists with ropes. They were dirty and tired, but I was so happy to see them I tried to hug and kiss one of them. He pushed me away roughly and pointed his rifle at me. Finding us in the Arrow Cross headquarters, they thought we belonged to the Arrow Cross. I tried to explain to them that we were Jewish and were only there because we were trying to stay alive, but they didn't understand Hungarian and we spoke no Russian.

They kept saying, "Fascist, Fascist!" and we kept saying, "No, No!" and tried to explain with hands and feet. In minutes we were surrounded by more Russian soldiers and by some of the people who lived there. When the Russians said "Fascist!" the people said, "Da, Da!" because they had seen us associate with the Arrow Cross. Finally an officer arrived. Crying, I drew him a Jewish star, and then I mimicked putting it on and then tearing it off and hiding. He understood and they let us go. And that's how the horrors we had lived through ended. It was hard to believe, but the war was over and we were still alive. On the evening of the 24th of December I received a new lease on life.

The Russians had liberated Budateteny, but it took them three more weeks before they could enter Budapest. The Germans had destroyed all the bridges leading to Budapest and the Russians had to build pontoons to cross the Danube. Then they had to fight from house to house to liberate Pest. In the meantime there were no food supplies. Everybody was hungry. One day we saw people cutting up a frozen horse that had died on the street. We asked for a piece and took it home and cooked it. It tasted strangely sweet, and not very good, but we ate it.

Once late in the afternoon, we heard the landlady scream for help. Some Russian soldiers entered and were trying to rape her. Our room was in the back and had a separate entrance. There was no way we could help her, so we ran away. A few houses down, we knocked on the door of a big house owned by an old couple. We told them what was happening and asked them to hide us. We could hear noise and Russian words even as we were speaking.

They took us to their bedroom, where there were two beds with large feather covers. They opened up the covers by folding them in two lengthwise, and we hid under the doubled up part of the covers against the wall. The Russians, ostensibly searching for food and drink, looked in the bedroom, but the beds looked empty. We were lucky again. After the soldiers left the old man brought in a big smoked ham and announced, "We are now going to eat this to make sure it goes into our stomachs," and he invited us for dinner.

After that we stayed with them. They gave Eva and me one of the beds to sleep in. The two of them slept in the other bed.

Russian Command Post

The next morning the Russian soldiers seized the house and turned it into the command post of the Russian corps of engineers. They installed their office in the front, in a large dining room. Eva, I, and the old people were allowed to stay. It was a big house with many rooms. The Russian officers were mostly engineers who were engaged in building bridges. At first we told them that we were Jews, escaping from the Germans, and knew nobody there. Later we learned not to volunteer the information that we were Jews because some of them were anti-Semitic.

There were also many Russian soldiers who, just passing through, used the house just to rest up a bit. We befriended the few of them that stayed there continuously and in the weeks that followed we learned some Russian from them. Since they were intelligent and educated people, we didn't feel endangered by them.

One day I asked an officer who had been friendly to me to look up my sister Fajgi, if possible, the next time he was in Pest and tell her that I was alive and well. A few days later when he returned, smiling, he handed me a letter from her. He told me that he had gone to her address, had talked to her, and she was fine. At first I couldn't believe it, but the letter, in Fajgi's handwriting, convinced me that it was true.

I thanked him, weeping. I was very touched by his gesture. Pest was still a battleground. He had risked his life to reassure me that my sister was alive. He just smiled and told me he'd do anything for me, and when the war was over that he would come back for me, marry me, and take me with him to Russia. That was more than I bargained for, but he was serious. He ordered his subordinates to take care of me and look out for me when he wasn't there, which was often. He told us not to leave the house for a few more days until the occupying forces could re-establish order.

The house was cold. The dining room, which served as the command post, was the only heated room. To keep warm we stayed there during the day. But when, with the aid of big maps, they made plans, they sent us out because by now we understood Russian pretty well.

More troops kept arriving, including many female soldiers. They rested for a few hours and then went on. Sometimes there were so many soldiers sleeping on the floor we couldn't move.

One evening all the Russians left and the house was completely empty. There was no bathroom and Eva and I hadn't washed for weeks. We warmed up water in the kitchen, took it to our room and took a bath in a basin. We had been wearing the same long pants all day and sleeping in them at night, too. So we decided to wash our pants also and we put them in the kitchen to dry. Because we were cold we got into our bed and then we fell asleep. In the morning the bridge builders returned while we were still asleep. When "my" officer saw our clothes hanging in the kitchen, he flew into a rage. He burst into our room, screaming and speaking so fast I understood only half of what he was saying. The gist of it was that we should not have gotten undressed because it was behavior enticing to any soldier that might be passing by. Finally, he left and we got dressed. I went to the dining room and tried to explain to him that the house had been empty, and we needed to wash our clothes sometimes. He continued raving. Suddenly he took out his revolver and shot at me. The bullet whistled by my ear. Terrified, I picked up the glass ashtray from the table and threw it at him. I got him square in the face and that brought him to himself. He was bleeding, but he paid no attention to it. He couldn't believe that he almost killed me. Weeping, he said he was sorry over and over. He said that he had not wanted to hurt me. Finally Eva took him to the kitchen and cleaned up his face and stopped the bleeding.

Home

On January 18, 1945, Budapest was liberated and everybody in the house set out in different directions. Eva and I went to Pest to look for our families. I went to the Wagner's house, on Ajtosi Dhurer Lane, where my sister was. She had already left them. She had told them she was Jewish and now that the war was over, she was going home. Mrs. Wagner was surprised. Mr. Wagner told her that he had known it for a long time. Fajgi had left me a message saying that she was at the house of her friend Zelma, waiting for me to set out for home. The streets were filled with frozen corpses. There were so many there hadn't been enough time to carry them away so they were deposited in front of the houses where people walked by them indifferently. By the time I got to Zelma's house, it was evening. There were many others there, getting ready to go home. I can't describe the joy I felt when I saw my sister. We held each other and cried.

The next day I went to the Levais' house on Vilmos Csaszar Street to get some of my clothes. Mr. and Mrs. Levai was there. There was no trace and no news of their son. Their son-in-law was dead. A few days before the liberation, the Arrow Cross entered the hospital where he had been hiding and first tortured and then massacred everyone there—doctors, nurses, patients. Mr. and Mrs. Levai were getting ready to move to Australia. They said they wanted nothing more to do with the hell of a country that Hungary had turned out to be.

I went to the bakery where my brother Szruel had worked, but he wasn't there and nobody knew anything about him.

Fajgi and I started walking home on January 22, 1945, early in the morning with a group of boys and girls. It was snowing heavily. We were carrying all our belongings on our backs. We were elated to be going home. The roads were full of people. Everybody was going someplace and since the trains weren't running yet, everybody was walking on the highway. At one point the Russians stopped us and detained the boys for work, but the rest of us kept walking.

In the afternoon a group of young men with a horse-drawn sled caught up with us. They asked us who we were and where we were going. We told them we were Jewish, and we were trying to get home. They were going home to Cegled from a labor camp. When one of them, Gasztonyi Pal, heard that our name was Katz and we were going to Szatmar, he said that he had been in camp with a Sandor Katz from Szatmar. They said that his friends called him Katzele, he was good at looking out for himself, and he was well liked. Our brother Zishu was alive!

Gasztonyi put our baggage on the sled and we walked on with them. Having some boys with us made us feel safer. We were on the road for a few days. At night we slept at peasant houses close to the road. When we got to Cegled, the mayor, who was Gasztonyi's friend, had a dinner made in his honor and Fajgi and I were invited. It had been a long time since I had eaten anything that delicious, sitting down at a beautifully set table with people around me. We sat at the table talking till late at night. Everybody had a story to tell.

In the morning, Gasztonyi asked the mayor to take us to the Russian command post to get us identification papers so that we would not have any problems during the rest of our journey. The papers, which said in both Hungarian and Russian that we were refugees on our way to our home town,

Szatmar, were useful. We had to identify ourselves many times in the next few days.

From Cegled we walked to Szolnok, hoping that the trains would be running from there. When we arrived, we found that the passenger trains weren't running yet, but we were able to climb onto the cattle car of a freight train. It was slow going. The train stopped at every little town to give the right of way to military trains. We shivered for days, sitting on the little straw that was in the cattle car.

In Debrecen, we slept at a private house together with many other refugees. In Debrecen, things were back to normal. One could buy anything, and the trains were running. As we were walking on the street we saw Szruel, our little brother, walking towards us. We couldn't believe our eyes. But it was true: it was him and he was fine. My heart was jumping with joy and anxiety. Dear God, was it possible that everyone else was all right?

Szruli had a young girl with him. He said he couldn't come home with us yet because he had promised the girl that he would take her home and protect her. He said we shouldn't worry about him, that we should go on ahead, that he would follow us later. He also said his name wasn't Szruli anymore—we should call him Tibor. Fajgi had also decided to adopt the name Ibolya and was introducing herself as Ibolya to everybody on the way home.

Szruli had a little suitcase full of perfume which he was selling to the Russian soldiers who were drinking it because they were desperate for anything alcoholic. I asked him how much money he had. He had more than ten times as much as Fajgi and I together. I asked him for half of it. I could tell that he wasn't too happy about it, but he gave us half of his money without voicing any objections. We went to the station, hoping to catch a train to Szatmar. There was nothing going straight to Szatmar, but there was a train to Nagyvarad the next day. We spent another night at the crowded private house. There was a young woman from Szatmar there—Mrs. Burger, the Trebics' daughter, with a baby in her arms. There were also others who were going to Szatmar.

We got on the train early in the morning. It was already pretty full, but we found two places by the window. By the time the train left, it was so full there wasn't even standing room in the hallway. At each station more people squeezed on. Sitting by the window, looking at the glowing, snow-covered fields and the poles rushing by, I thought of my last trip, going in the other direction, on New Year's Eve the year before. Then it was in the middle of the night, and the train was deserted. The train had been running through the darkness and I had spent this past year in darkness. But now it was all over. It was daytime, the sun was shining, and the train was full of people going home. My heart was full of anticipation.

At Nagyvarad, we had to wait a few hours for our connection to Szatmar. I went to the hairdresser to have my hair washed and trimmed. I couldn't remember the last time I was able to have my hair done and I wanted to look good for Mamma. I sat down in the chair and the hairdresser put a white towel around my neck. But instead of doing my hair she exchanged horrified glances with her co-workers.

"What's wrong?" I asked.

"Miss," she said, "your hair is full of lice!"

I was surprised and embarrassed, but I wasn't going to let her know.

"Well, do something about it!" I said.

If she knew what I had just been through she wouldn't have been surprised that I had lice.

Full of anticipation, we got on the train to Szatmar late in the afternoon. We were going home! We would be home soon! We thanked God to have lived long enough to see this day.

Then we were home and there was nobody there.

The only piece of furniture left in our five-room apartment was the dining room table. It was too big and too heavy to be removed. I closed my eyes and could see us all sitting around the table on Friday nights, Father and the boys singing *zmires*, Mamma listening with a tired but happy smile. The extreme cold made my vision vanish. We were standing in an empty apartment, our hopes dashed. I remember thinking, "Dear God, where is everybody? Where is Mamma? Where are my brothers and sisters?"

We waited for a long time, but nothing happened, no one returned. We didn't know till later that they never would come. Our family, our neighbors, and most of the inhabitants of our city had been swallowed up by the gas chambers. Along with millions of others, they vanished into smoke. The only earthly thing left of Mamma, of my other brothers and sisters, and their children was the grease that clings to the sides of the crematorium smokestacks.

Father's grave

We had no money and no plans. We looked for the superintendent. She was there, in her apartment at the back of the yard. She used to start the fires for the tenants in the winter, on Saturday mornings. Now she was presiding over an empty building. She had a message for us. There had been several communications from the bank. One hundred dollars from Uncle Moritz were waiting at the bank for anyone in the Katz family.

We went to the cemetery and found Father's grave. His marker was just a piece of wood with his name on it: Aron, ben Itzhak Yankov ha Cohen. From far away, the sound of someone weeping bitterly and singing *eil mule rachamim* (a mourning hymn) was drifting over the snow-covered graves.

Russian and Hungarian I.D. paper

As Ilona Kirtag

With Erno Hollander

Above: With Negus
Below: Center with Laci Vamos

My parents with my three younger brothers and Fajgi

Uncle Moritz and Aunt Zsenka

My sister Malku and her two children

Chaim Zafir

My oldest sister, Perl

~ *Part Three* ~

AFTER THE WAR

Struggling

For a while it looked like we were the only two Jewish girls left in the entire city. In the next few days, we found that others had come home—mostly the young and unattached, and those who had been able to flee to other parts of Romania when Hungary occupied Transylvania in 1940, or who survived in the forced labor companies. Some social services had been established. A few returning young medical doctors reopened the Jewish hospital. The Jewish Community Relief Office was opened. It was supported financially by the JOINT (the American Jewish Joint Distribution Committee) with the purpose of offering financial aid to the homecoming survivors. The relief office also operated a soup kitchen. Another relief organization, the local Popular Defense Organization, run by the communists, had established an inventory of Jewish belongings either abandoned by Nazis who had fled when the Soviet and Romanian armies reoccupied the city or given to Nazi sympathizers.

We knew that Szruli and Zishu were alive. Szruli was escorting a young girl home across Hungary, and Zishu was waiting for his family in Budapest. Only Fajgi and I had come home to Szatmar. The walls, broken windows, and a table were all that was left of our home. Since the apartment wasn't fit to live in, we spent the first few days at the house of a Jewish man we met on the train on our way home. He and some members of his family had a furnished house and a housekeeper. We were welcome to stay there as long as we wanted, but we were in a hurry to get settled at home. We were waiting for other members of our family to return, and we wanted to be ready for them.

All we owned was the clothing we were wearing, the contents of our backpacks that we had brought from Hungary, and the one hundred dollars Uncle Moric sent us from America. We sought help from the Jewish Community Relief Office and were told that since we had not been deported we were not eligible for any help from them. We were very disappointed. I volunteered to help serve lunch and dinner at the soup kitchen, partly because the Jewish Community Relief Office was a clearing house of news of the missing and of people returning to their homes. There was a bulletin board where a list of new arrivals was posted daily. Surrounding the list were notes in which people asked for news of members of their families. "Does anyone know anything about…," they would begin. The notes multiplied daily, but the replies were few.

Every survivor had his own personal tragedy for which there was no consolation. Everyone had memories of lost loved ones, and their souls had festering wounds. In spite of it all, everyone tried to start again. Once-distant relatives now became close because it was vitally important for everyone to find someone to live with and to live for.

We applied for aid to the local Popular Defense Organization, which had taken over the administration, distribution, and, later, the liquidation of Jewish assets that had been held by the Nazis. The PDO considered us qualified as victims of the Nazis and they gave us a beautiful walnut furniture set made by Kalman Szucs, a famous Hungarian furniture maker. When the PDO learned that we could sew, we were given two small Singer sewing machines to make pillowcases and sheets for the hospital. A few weeks later, a woman who was in the leadership of the PDO found out that we received furniture made by Kalman Szucs. A member of the Communist Party, she had better connections than we did, and so nobody objected when she took the furniture from us. She told us that the furniture belonged to her family. She was lying. The Nazis did not take furniture from non-Jewish families. Not only that, she didn't realize that the sofa was part of the set. We kept it in a different room for me to sleep on, and she saw it there. We knew she was lying, but there was nothing we could do. She had the power to do as she liked. The PDO gave us the address of an abandoned apartment on the outskirts of the city where we could get another bedroom set. This was not as nice as the first one, but it didn't matter. A few months later someone else who had connections wanted it and it was taken from us.

Months passed, and no one else came home from our family. No one cared what happened to us. I had to give up volunteering at the soup kitchen because we needed to establish a source of income for our daily needs. The little money we had was melting away. I had hoped that, having made it home, life would be a little easier. I was not yet twenty years old. All my life I had skimped on food and had worked as hard as I could. I remember thinking that I should be able to act like other girls my age. I wanted to be carefree, pampered, going about with friends. I wanted someone else to take care of me. I didn't want to be the decision maker, the one responsible for everything. My wishes were not granted.

I had carried home from Budapest two small rolls of lingerie materials in my backpack. It was loot discarded by Russian soldiers. They had broken into stores, looking for alcoholic drinks. They drank anything containing alcohol— even shaving lotion and cologne, though they preferred vodka. They were also obsessed with obtaining wristwatches. I saw Russian soldiers wearing three or four wristwatches on their arms. Some even had wristwatches on their legs. I don't know if they were true, but people told stories of soldiers asking watchmakers to make wristwatches of large wall and alarm clocks. While searching for liquor and watches, they threw anything else they found on the store shelves into the street. I saw the two small rolls of lingerie material and held on to them. The material was very thin, so it didn't take up much room, but it was quite heavy. Now, working in our home, we made nightgowns and baby clothes from this material. Many of the survivors bought them as gifts for family members they were expecting to come home. As long as the material lasted, we made enough money to sustain us. When we had to buy new material, our income became quite limited. Many times my sister and I shared one meal because we didn't have enough money for two.

One evening I was taking made-to-order baby clothes to a neighbor in the building next to ours. From the verandah I noticed through the window a fire in the fireplace of a furnished room. I rang the bell—no answer. I tried the door. It was open. In the entry there were two doors. Instinctively I opened the door to the room I had seen from the verandah. The room was dark and it seemed to be empty. The flickering flames drew strange shadows on the walls. I started at the sound of a voice from the dark side of the room. There, when my eyes got used to the dark, I saw a young man sitting alone, his face streaked with tears.

"How can I help you?" he asked in a hesitant voice, while wiping his face with a handkerchief.

"I am looking for Mrs. Loerinc," I said, embarrassed to have surprised him in his sorrow.

"They aren't home yet," he said, turning on the lights.

"I brought her some things we made for her baby," I said.

"They should be home any time now. You can wait here if you like," he said, offering a chair. "Or you can leave the things, if you prefer."

I took the chair and sat near the fireplace. I wanted to

know who he was. I had been at Mrs. Loerinc's before and had never seen him there. In addition, I was deeply moved by his unhappiness and wanted to keep him company.

"My name is Sanyi Farkas."

"I am Rozsi Katz. My sister and I are living in the next house at number four."

"This house belongs to my cousin. I actually helped build it. My cousin's husband was called to the labor service while the house was under construction. I am much younger than he was and wasn't called in till two years later. I supervised the construction till the house was finished."

So he, too, was a survivor. The next question, "Where were you during the war?" was inevitable. In those days, whenever two survivors met, as soon as they realized that they were both survivors the next question was always, "Where were you during the war?" And always, the need to talk about what we went through fought within us with the need to say nothing, to not relive the horrors in the retelling.

This is an agony which has not been lessened by the passage of time. It is now fifty years later, and still, whenever we meet other survivors, whatever the circumstances, the conversation inevitably turns to what happened to us during the war, even though most of us would prefer not to talk about it. Every survivor has his own personal tragedy. There was, and is, no consolation. The things that happened cannot be changed, and talking about them does not help. Still, we cannot forget the loss of our loved ones. The memories are bleeding wounds which cannot ever heal. The events we remember branded our souls with a red-hot iron.

But at that time, I didn't know all this. I didn't yet fully appreciate the extent of our losses and their collective impact. I only knew that I was eager to hear the stranger's story. We talked for a long time and agreed to meet again so we could talk some more.

He had returned home from labor service a few days earlier and discovered that his parents' house had been bombed. He was staying at his cousin's house because he had nowhere else to go. He was hoping his sister was alive. He had seen a notice that she was on her way home, but hadn't arrived yet. (She must have perished on the way home because she never did return.) He didn't know yet if the cousin was alive. (The cousin's husband died at Bori.)

Slowly, over the next few months, his need to talk won out over his shrinking back from the horrors he lived through, and Sanyi told me the story of how he survived the war. The following is his story, in his words.

Sanyi's Story

I was drafted to serve in labor company 110/67 in the winter of 1943. At first our regiment was at Nagy Banya (Baia Mare). From there we were directed to Szatmar. The freight train carrying our company arrived in the station at Szatmar just as the last transport to Auschwitz was being prepared for loading. Our train was shunted to the edge of the station, out of sight of the Auschwitz transport and adjacent to the cemetery. We saw some commotion in front—gendarmes, policemen, and the SS were coming and going everywhere. German and Hungarian military trains loaded with tanks and canons waited to leave, and others arrived and departed. We didn't know what was going on. Our guards had strict instructions not to let us wander about. The station and even the front of our train were out of bounds.

A few boys and I stole away to visit the cemetery. I wanted to see my father's grave. I am a Cohen and am not permitted to go inside a cemetery. I looked through the little window in the fence in front of his grave, which is next to my grandmother's. I said a prayer, and asked someone who was inside to hand me a wildflower I saw growing on my father's burial plot. I wanted something from my father to take with me. I pressed it in my notebook to save it. Today, fifty years later, I still have it.

The last transport

After waiting hours in the station, we were unloaded and directed to the outskirts of the city. At the same time, deportees were being herded toward the train station. We were not supposed to meet, but the authorities in charge of the deportations miscalculated the timing. As we were about to cross the bridge over the Szamos River, a group of Jewish people—mostly older men, women, and children, carrying bundles and suitcases—appeared on a side street. We stopped to take in this wave of human misery. When they realized what had happened, our surprised guards hurriedly led us away at gun point. As long as I live, the sight of those frightened faces will haunt me. At the end of the group, sitting on the side of a flatcar pulled by a scrawny horse, was the Rosh Bet Din (the chief of the Ritual Court), an old man who had been respected by all Szatmar for his wisdom. Long white beard, a shiny black caftan and black hat, eyes staring into emptiness, he was the vision of a saint.

We were rushed to temporary quarters, where we stayed a couple of days, while a small part of the ghetto set aside for us was fenced off. The first day in the ghetto, many of us jumped the fence after work to look for where our families had stayed. At the front of a small house I recognized a white bench that we used to keep on our verandah. Inside were three empty rooms—no furniture, just things spread all over the floor. On the stove in the kitchen I found pots and pans with partially prepared or burnt food. The people who had lived there obviously had been forced to leave at a moment's notice. It was dark inside. I didn't recognize any personal belongings of my mother or my sister. Yet I knew without a shadow of a doubt that this was the last place they had lived in Szatmar. I stayed for a long time hoping that, somehow, breathing the air they had breathed a short while ago would connect me with them. It was evening when I left, carrying the weight of a millstone on my chest.

From Szatmar we were directed to Kolozsvar (Cluj), where we stayed about a month. We worked in the ghetto for a short time, gathering and sorting the things left behind. I believe that this assignment was our commandant's doing. He was one of those rare officers who behaved humanely when inhumanity was the norm. He regarded us as unfortunate victims of the times, and tried to make life easier for us. Working in the ghetto enabled many to find warm clothes and blankets. There were some boys who had had no blankets at all.

From Kolozsvar our company was transferred to Budapest. We were quartered at 33 Bencur Street in a bombed area of the city. Our assignment was to clean up rubble and, at the Feri Hill airport, to fill in bomb craters. The latter task proved to be in vain, since every day at noon the shiny silver airplanes of the Allies appeared in the skies above the city and bombed everything. At 11:30 everybody in the airport—civilians, workers, and soldiers—ran to the cornfields surrounding the airfield. Realizing that we were witnessing their helplessness, those in charge transferred us to Csanad, a little Slavonic village outside Budapest, to dig tank traps for the city's defense.

We were quartered in peasant houses in one part of the vil-
lage. The villagers were not Nazi sympathizers and they treated
us kindly. It was harvest time. On Sundays I helped the old peas-
ant and his wife in whose house I was lodged with the field work.
We shared our lunches and put in a good day's work.

At the end of October 1944, after Szalasi's Arrow Cross Party
came to power, the village was suddenly packed with Arrow Cross
guards who brought civilians, mostly teenage children and
women, to help with the digging. One evening after we came
home from work, the peasant locked the door and gathered to-
gether those of us quartered in his house. A pleasant odor of spicy
roast filled the small room. "I killed the little pig. Better that we
eat it before the Arrow Cross requisitions it," he said, smiling, as
he invited us to the table. This was the first time I ate pork, and I
felt uneasy. But we all were hungry and the roast tasted very
good.

Having seen a lot of bombing in Budapest, my labor contin-
gent was used to air raids. We were familiar with the effects of
huge, small, and cluster bombs. We were accustomed to the hellish
flashing of explosions, the frenetic fireworks of red-hot bullets
crisscrossing the dark skies. We were not bothered much, and we
were pleased to see how frightened were the gendarmes, who were
so "brave and courageous" while mistreating old people and
women and children.

One night in this little village, I saw a ferocious air raid, the
likes of which I had not encountered before. It started as usual
with sirens howling. We turned over and tried to go back to sleep.
Suddenly a light that seemed brighter than sunshine flooded the
area for miles. Grabbing our clothes, we hurried outside. It was
amazing. In complete silence, floating in the sky high above us,
there was a device that looked like a lighted Christmas tree. The
searchlight beams paled in the brightness of this unnatural light.
There wasn't much time to wonder. The loud roar of the ap-
proaching bombers broke the stillness, and small incendiary bombs

fell like rain. Some looked like fiery spears. Others exploded on impact, spreading bright yellow flames everywhere. It seemed like the whole village, from the sky to the ground, was on fire. The whistle of falling bombs was everywhere. We thought each bomb's trajectory was just overhead and that every one was going to hit us. People panicked and ran in all directions. Then, like a passing thunderstorm, it was all over. The roaring airplanes departed, and the whistling and the explosions ceased. All was quiet and dark again. Only the crackling of a distant fire could be heard. Just a few minutes earlier, the whole world had seemed to be on fire. We could see in the distance that a heavily guarded military installation, possibly a depot, between the village and the city was in flames. Two or three village houses that were closest to the city had also been hit and were burning. The next day we were told to stay in our quarters. All day we saw soldiers marching and German troops in covered trucks driving to Budapest. The Arrow Cross disappeared from the village.

Soon after that our company was ordered back to Budapest. There were rumors of deportations of both civilians and labor companies to Germany. We were frightened. Civilians, even young girls, came to hide for a night or a day in our lodgings. Our commandant closed his eyes and ordered the cooks to feed everybody.

The frightening rumors of deportations persisted. I was in the same labor company with three cousins: Laycsi Friedman, who was my age (twenty); and Jeno, Laycsi's older brother (Laycsi and Jeno were both sons of one of my mother's brothers); and Miska Grosinger, also twenty, who was a son of Laycsi's and Jeno's mother's sister. Jeno discovered that another cousin, Dr. Rabbi Sanyi Grosinger, who had been the chief Conservative rabbi of Debrecen, was in Budapest. He was now a Swiss citizen working in the personnel office of the International Red Cross.

We contacted him, and he suggested that we escape from the labor company. To the four of us and Jeno's friend, Zoltan Roz, he gave Red Cross armbands and ID papers identifying us as Red

Cross employees working in a Red Cross orphanage at 32 Akacfa Street. I'll never forget the day when the five of us left the labor camp, marching in the middle of the street with our rucksacks on our backs and the Red Cross armbands on our arms. We were trembling inside, but nobody stopped us. We looked like a Red Cross detail going on a mission.

At the orphanage we were received by the director, Mr. Polnai, a tall, impressive-looking old man with white hair and a thick white mustache. After the First World War, he had been the commerce minister of Hungary, and everybody still addressed him as "Your Excellency." Dr. Grosinger had told him to expect us, and he was happy to see us. He needed our help, and even more than our help, he needed the connection to the International Red Cross.

The orphanage at 32 Akacfa Street was in the ghetto. Initially it was a small institution—a few common bedrooms, a large kitchen, a dining room, and a couple of offices, all on the first floor. Lately, because so many adults had been swallowed by the war, it had become the improvised home to several hundred children from three to ten years old.

It occupied a three-story apartment house. A large, heavy oak gate in the center of the building led through a hallway to a courtyard surrounded on all sides by the complex. Two staircases, one on each side of the hallway, led to the second and third floors. Individual apartments were entered from balconies with iron railings, which ran around the upper floors of the building. The ground floor had contained stores, now closed. A huge hall at the front of the second floor had been a dance school with a shiny parquet floor, but in the last couple of years it had served as quarters for a forced labor company that had been deported to Germany a few days before we arrived. Now the whole building was occupied by the orphanage and its forty-five employees, who all lived on the premises.

My cousins and I were quartered in a two-bedroom apartment on the third floor. Mr. Polnai outlined our duties: Jeno, who

knew how to type, was assigned to the office and the others became aides doing all kinds of necessary jobs. I volunteered to go
with William Fisher, the husband of one of the cooks, to collect ra-
tions for the orphanage—bread from a bakery, and groceries, vegetables, meat, and other supplies from warehouses of the Red
Cross. Willi needed help with the little flat four-wheel handcart
and I was curious to see the city. The others were smarter and
preferred to stay on the premises.

Willi was from Budapest and knew his way around. We
bought ourselves caps similar to those worn by the Arrow Cross.
With the caps and the armbands as our armor, several times a
week we collected food from all over Budapest. One morning not
long after we arrived at the orphanage, gendarmes, the Arrow
Cross, and Nazi officials ordered all men and women working in
the orphanage between the ages of eighteen and forty to take their
most necessary personal belongings and follow them to Klouzal
Place, which was nearby. At Klouzal Place we found thousands of
people lined up, five in a row, in groups of fifty, in preparation
for being marched to the railroad station from where they would
be deported to Germany. The five of us managed to stay together.
We were waiting for our group to be formed, resigned to our fate.
Suddenly, Mr. Polnai appeared. With his bow tie, long white
hair, and mustache, he was the very picture of a Hungarian aristocrat. He really was an aristocrat, who just happened to be Jewish. He had obtained an official document delivered by special
messenger and signed by Prime Minister Szalasi stating that the
children and all the personnel of the Akacfa Street International
Red Cross Orphanage were exempted from the laws concerning
the Jews and that they were under the protection of the Arrow
Cross Party. A notarized list of the employees signed by Dr.
Grosinger, Chief of the Personnel Division of the International
Red Cross Delegation of Budapest, was attached. One by one, our
names were called, and we marched back to the orphanage.

Willi and I had many other encounters with police and the
Arrow Cross. Our Red Cross IDs served us well and saved us

several times. On one occasion we were picked up by a gang of the Arrow Cross and taken to the Danube River steps to be shot. We, along with a large number of people plucked from the streets, were lined up on the lowest step. The leader of the Arrow Cross was haranguing us. He was just about finished, for he was screaming, "Say your last prayers, you f—— Jews," when a platoon of policemen, led by an officer of high rank, surrounded them. The Arrow Cross had been so absorbed in their enjoyable game with us that they didn't see the policemen until it was too late. The policemen disarmed the Arrow Cross. The police officer, not deigning to look at the Arrow Cross chief, shouted in outrage, "Where are we? Aren't there laws in this country anymore? Can anybody take the law into his own hands?" He descended the steps to the river and asked each person why he had been detained. Some he dismissed on the spot. Others he ordered to line up at the top of the steps some distance from the water. When he approached Willi and me, we showed him our Red Cross IDs and the order to pick up the supplies. His face red with anger, he swore at the Arrow Cross: "You ————s! Don't you know that the Red Cross aids our wounded soldiers at the front? You are violating international law by detaining Red Cross employees!" Turning to us he shouted, "Step down." He didn't have to tell us twice. We left without looking back.

For a few days Willi and I were both in shock and didn't dare leave the orphanage. But supplies were short. The children and employees had to be fed, and there was no one else to fetch supplies. We needed to build up reserves to last through what we knew were the last days of the war. With Dr. Grosinger's help we proceeded to amass canned food, dried beans, barley, and wheat-mush.

One day near the end of December on Kiraly Street, Willi was pulling and I was pushing the cart when an air raid sounded. We didn't stop for air raids. It was safer on the streets for us during an air raid than at other times because the Arrow Cross goons hid in the shelters. As we were approaching the ghetto, shrapnel hit

Willi. He fell on the ground screaming in pain. When I looked at his wound, I almost fainted. The shrapnel had cut off a piece of his left thigh. The wound did not bleed, but through the raw flesh I could see the bone. I picked Willi up and ran to the make-shift hospital in the school building just outside the ghetto. He was heavy. By the time I arrived he was unconscious, and I was exhausted and terrified.

The scene inside was a setting from Dante's Inferno. People lay in the hallways on stretchers or on the bare floor, some screaming in pain, some dying. From inside the operating rooms came the sound of gruesome howling. Doctors were operating without anesthetic. Because our Red Cross arm bands gave us some priority, I was able to take Willi directly to the first operating room. On a teacher's desk covered with a bloody sheet a young doctor, helped by two nurses, was operating on a person in bandages who was moaning in pain. I put Willi down on an empty stretcher and left. I was sure that if I stayed another minute I would faint. I never saw Willi again and I don't know what happened to him. To this day I have frequent nightmares of the hallway of the hospital. After Willi's accident neither I nor anybody else from the orphanage left the ghetto until the end of the war.

Remnants of Our Family

My sister and I worked long and hard to support ourselves. There was no one to help us. One day our brother Zishu, now called Sandor, sent us word that he was in Arad and that he would be coming to Szatmar soon. The messenger was a friend of our brother's who told us that Sandor had a grocery store in Budapest with a partner whose sister he had married. The trip to Arad combined their honeymoon with an occasion to barter fur coats and other things he had brought with him for sugar, food stuffs, salt, and other goods that were hard to find in Budapest after the war. According to the messenger, my brother was doing quite well financially.

I went to Arad to meet my brother and his new wife, Teresa, and together we traveled to Szatmar. Teresa, whose mother, brother, and friends all lived in Budapest, didn't want to settle in Szatmar. So after staying a few days they went back to Budapest. In May 1946, they had a son named Ervin.

While Teresa was expecting a baby, they heard from a former neighbor, who had been in the Bergen-Belsen concentration camp, that Eva, Sandor's daughter from his previous marriage, had survived. She had been taken to an orphanage in Sweden. It took Sandor and Teresa two years to cut through all the bureaucratic tangles, but finally, in 1947, with the help of the International Red Cross, Eva was reunited with her father in Budapest.

Our parents' apartment, with three of the rooms empty, was too big for just my sister Ibi and me, and living there reminded us constantly of family who were still missing. We decided to move. We found a two-bedroom apartment with a small kitchen and an entry hall at 1 Kazincy Street, a big elegant apartment house in the center of the town across from the central park. Originally occupied by wealthy Jewish families, the apartments had been given to Nazis and German officers, and after the war they had been abandoned. Some of them were pretty thoroughly vandalized. The one we chose was empty and in relatively good shape. We made the smaller room into our sewing shop, furnishing it with our sewing machines, a table, and a couple of chairs which we had found in another apartment. We lived in the other room.

We worked long and hard to squeeze out a living for both of us. Shortly after we moved in, a Communist Party delegate took away one of our sewing machines. Left with one sewing machine, my sister Ibi cut and sewed while I did the hand finishing, trimming, and pressing.

In May 1945, Nazi Germany was defeated, and the war

was finally over. One by one, the three husbands of my older sisters came home. First Avrum Gluck, then Shulem Fried, and lastly Chaim Zafir arrived. Chaim told us that he, my sister Malku, their two children, my mother, and my two younger brothers had been in the same cattle car when they were deported. Mamma, he told us, had prayed *thilem* all during that miserable trip. In Auschwitz a small, careless motion of Dr. Mengele's hand ordered all of them, except Chaim, to the line on the left. That was the line to the gas chambers. Not one of my three older sisters nor any of their children survived.

Avrum remained in town a few months. Then he left to join relatives elsewhere in Romania. He never wrote us and we lost touch. Shulem remarried and in the spring of 1948 emigrated to Israel. He and his wife have four children and twelve grandchildren. Chaim too remarried, and by the time he and his family were able to emigrate to Israel in 1958, he had five children. They had four more children in Israel and they have grandchildren. Occasionally we hear from both of the families.

The Groza Train

Survivors continued to arrive daily. Sick and weak, most of them looked like living skeletons. They spoke of others still in Poland and Germany who barely clung to life in hospitals or who had recovered from typhus but didn't have the strength to come home. In response to pleas from survivors and the Jewish Community Council of Varad (Oradea), Romania's Prime Minister, Petru Groza, sent a train to Poland and Germany to collect these people. The train was staffed by four people: Sanyi Fried from Kolozsvar (Cluj), who had been in the same labor service unit with Sanyi Farkas; Miklos Sarkany from Szatmar, who was a friend of ours; another labor camp survivor from Varad whose name we don't remember; and a young woman who spoke Russian. Equipped with blankets, medicines, and canned food, the train left Varad and arrived at Auschwitz three days later. Miklos Sarkany hoped to find his mother in a hospital there. He had arranged to volunteer because on a trip to a city near Szatmar, two women stopped him on the street and told him that his mother had been alive when Auschwitz was liberated. He spent those three days and three nights mentally pushing the locomotive to make it go faster. To his sorrow, he arrived too late. He didn't find his mother, but he stayed on with the train, which made two more trips, the last one in May 1945. Local Jewish Community Councils directed to them the survivors who needed help going home.

It was a dangerous time to travel. The war wasn't officially over yet. There were no laws observed or enforced. Several times the Russians tried to confiscate the train, claiming the papers documenting their humanitarian mission were not official. On one occasion, despite pleading that the lives of most of those on the train depended on getting them home and under the care of doctors quickly, they were all forced to get off the train. While begging and negotiating with the Russian officers, they managed to get them so drunk that, with the help of the station master, they escaped with the train. From then on they always carried liquor to bribe their way through Eastern Europe.

The train met many other examples of inhumanity and greed but also of exceptional courage. On one return trip from Auschwitz, the train stopped at a town in Poland to allow everybody to rest overnight. The engineer, the railroad personnel, and those who were well enough to walk spent the night in a small hotel across from the station. In the middle of the night the stationmaster roused them. A rumor had spread that there were Jews on the train who planned to settle in the town. The townspeople, worried that the Jews planned to repossess property they had lost when they were deported, were planning a pogrom. They were prepared to kill the Jews to hold on to their unlawfully acquired possessions. The stationmaster, risking his life to warn them, urged them to leave immediately before any blood was shed. He arranged for an emergency right of way. The Groza train left before the mob arrived. Jews who had lived through the hell of the concentration camps were still running for their lives.

Tibi

Not long after my brother Sandor and his wife Teresa left for Budapest, Szruel, now Tibi, came home. We engaged him as an apprentice in an upholstery shop, but he was unexcited about his prospects in that job. In the fall of 1946, we decided it would be better if he joined Sandor in Budapest. After all, Sandor was the oldest, he was doing well financially, and he was better able than two young girls to take care of a teenage boy. But Sandor and Teresa had a baby and Teresa's mother lived with them in a two-bedroom apartment. They had no place to put up Tibi.

Tibi found friends from his earlier stay in Budapest who were preparing to emigrate legally—or, if necessary, illegally—to Palestine, and Tibi decided to join them. I was heartbroken. What was left of our family was drifting apart.

Tibi spent a long time at a training camp in Hungary. From there he was transferred to another military training camp in the Italian Alps. In the spring of 1948 he left for Palestine, landing in Haifa in May, just a few days before the Declaration of Independence. Twenty years old, he was immediately taken into the army. He fought in the War of Independence until he was severely wounded in his neck and right arm. It wasn't clear if he was going to pull through. Too sick to write himself, he asked someone else to write us of what had happened to him. He spent two years in various hospitals, but he recovered. During all this time, defying the communist regime's disapproval, we wrote him as often as we could. Later he told us that our letters kept him going.

After his recovery Tibi settled in a little village. He bought a wagon and two horses and made a living by making deliveries in the village and to the nearby city. Tibi had not fully recovered, however, and this work proved to be too strenuous. He sold the wagon and horses and got a job in a textile mill, where he learned to operate a power loom. He worked there until 1965, when he emigrated to the USA, where once again we were united.

I Fall in Love

Meanwhile, my sister and I became good friends with Sanyi. He now visited us daily. The commander of the Russian occupying forces and a few other officers had their private quarters in Sanyi's cousin's house. Deciding that they needed the whole house, they ordered all civilians in the house to move. So Sanyi moved to our building at 1 Kazincy Street. He worked at the Russian Army grain and produce quota warehouse. Every village had to bring an imposed quota of produce and grain to this warehouse, and from there it was shipped by train to supply centers. After work he spent most of his free time with us. Although I kept asking him to tell us more about his experiences in Budapest, he evaded my questions. He didn't like to talk about those events. I didn't get the whole story until years later and it came out in bits and pieces.

Sanyi became a reliable friend. We turned to him if we needed advice. We discussed our daily problems and worries with him. I didn't think of him as a boyfriend. He was serious and didn't know how to dance, while I loved to laugh and to dance. He just wasn't my type. Many times, when I saw him coming through the entry, I left through the kitchen. Though he had come to see me, he didn't seem to mind keeping Ibi company.

And then as time passed I got to know him better and fell in love with him. He introduced me to what was left of his family, told me stories of his childhood, and was a gentleman. He did not speak of marriage.

Mikola

One Sunday Sanyi and his cousin Laycsi Friedman invited me to go with them to visit their family in Mikola, a little village about ten miles from Szatmar. We hired a carriage and the three of us set off. It was a beautiful, sunny day. There were no people or cars on the road, which wound through green or freshly plowed fields. A soft breeze carried the scent of plowed earth and hay. Fleecy white clouds were swimming peacefully in the light blue sky. Except for the rhythmic clinks of the horseshoes and the grinding of the wheels on the gravel, all was quiet. The horse, the driver, and the three of us seemed to be the only living things in the world. Just outside Mikola, we drove through an old forest where, on an intersecting trail, we met peasant children with baskets full of mushrooms and berries.

The main street of the village was a long, dirt road. Two or three narrow sidestreets branched off from it. On both sides of the dusty road, ditches for rainwater runoff separated the road from the sidewalks. The sidewalks were paved with large flat stones. Whitewashed picket or plank fences guarded the front yards of the well-tended peasant houses. In front of the houses, flowers stretched their multi-colored blooms to the sunshine, and green vines crept up the porch posts.

We drove to the very end of the village. The last house was a manor. A large, fenced orchard separated it from the neighbor's house to the left, and to the right, behind a row of acacia trees, were vast fields. In front of the house were a

Driving through the forest

huge flower garden and a large verandah curtained with thick vines. We crossed a little bridge to the manor gates, and drove down a driveway bordered by ornamental trees, flower beds, and rose trees. We got out of the carriage, and stretched after the long drive.

"This is the house of my Uncle Sandor, Laycsi's father," Sanyi told me. "This is the place where I spent all my summer vacations from as far back as I can remember until I was a teenager." Mikola was the village where Sanyi's mother's family, the Friedmans, had lived for hundreds of years. Jews were not allowed to live in the city of Szatmar yet when the Friedmans first settled in Mikola. In the graveyard in Mikola there is a four-hundred-year-old tombstone of a Friedman. The Friedmans prospered in Mikola, and became well known. Even those of the family who moved to other places were always known as the "Friedmans from Mikola."

Two of Laycsi's brothers, Jozsi and Zoli, came out of the house to greet us. Before the deportations there had been eight siblings, four brothers and four sisters. None of the sisters came back from Auschwitz. They had had small children with them, which made survival out of the question. The four brothers survived. Jeno and Laycsi, who had escaped with Sanyi from the labor company in Budapest, lived in Szatmar, while Jozsi and Zoli were trying to rebuild the farm. Jozsi and Zoli had married two sisters from the same village. Sanyi knew the girls from before the war and was happy to see that they had survived and had become his relatives. Everybody was trying to start over, to build a family from ruins.

Sanyi's Stories of Mikola

"Uncle Sandor's house holds the happiest memories of my life. Uncle Sandor was Laycsi's father." He went on, overwhelmed by memories.

I spent all my summer vacations here from as far back as I can remember. During the school year my girl cousins used to live in our house so that they could go to high school in Szatmar. The boys traveled to Szatmar daily by train to go to high school. In the summer, for three or four weeks I stayed at Uncle Sandor's house or with the rest of the family in Mikola. Zaydi (grandfather) and Bubby (Grandma) lived in a large house in the middle of the village. There was a grocery store and a pub and grain warehouses behind the house. Zaydi and Bubby had four sons and two daughters. Uncle Sandor was the oldest. Next came Uncle Dezsö, Aunt Ilonka, Uncle Kalman, and my mother, who was the youngest. Uncle Adolph died when he was a young man, so I am not sure where he fit in between his siblings. Except for my mother and Uncle Kalman, who lived in Szatmar, they all lived in Mikola. Aunt Ilonka and her husband Uncle Moritz lived in Zaydi's house. Zaydi was a successful businessman and Uncle Moritz took over the business when he and Bubby got too old for it. Aunt Ilonka and Uncle Moritz didn't have children. They always wanted me to stay with them, but I didn't like to be the only child there. It was much more fun at Uncle Sandor's house, where there were lots of children. Uncle Dezsö had three girls and two boys, of whom a boy and a girl were about the same age as I. Sometimes I also stayed with them. Of my thirteen cousins, only six came back from the war.

When I was child, Uncle Sandor's house was bustling with life. Now the stables, sheds, and sheep barn are empty. Even the furniture had been stolen from the house during the war.

Wherever I turn, wherever I look, something reminds me of my childhood. The coach shed! It used to house a shiny black coach. I would sit in the driver's seat, driving pretend horses to unknown, faraway places.

At home, even during the summer, I had to go for half a day to cheder (Hebrew school), but in Mikola I was on vacation. Since my cousins had to go to cheder in the morning, I was often alone, but I was never bored. I could play and entertain myself for hours. I climbed the trees in the orchard, sat on the wagons or the farming equipment in the farmyard, and checked out the bake house and a small room full of brood-hens sitting on eggs that opened from it. Just being here was exciting for a city boy like me.

Once I was in Mikola during spring vacation. The snow had just melted. Everything was fresh and green, the scent of the blossoms of the fruit trees filled the air. The shepherd was in the sheep barn busy with the new-born lambs and he let me pick some up. They were warm, their fur white and soft.

In the evenings the farmyard bustled with activity. The milk cows and buffaloes, returning from the pasture with the village herd, filled every yard. The farm workers came back from far away fields on horses or in wagons pulled by oxen or buffalo. My Uncle Sandor had seven hundred acres of farmland, some of it quite far away. The workers would start at dawn and in the evening everyone was happy the day was over. During the day the yard was taken over by the poultry. Except for a dog chasing a cat or the rooster's crowing, everything was quiet.

Uncle Sandor's wife, Aunt Zseni, raised a flock of turkeys every summer. She was a famous housekeeper. At her table, besides the ten of them, there were always three or four family and business guests.

I remember one late summer evening, during harvest time. My uncle hired some migrant Romanian peasants as harvest workers. They brought their wives and children with them. They worked in teams, one man with a scythe followed in turn by a swath-layer, a person with a sickle gathering heaps, the binder tying the heaps in sheaves with straw rope, and finally the one who carried and built crosses from the sheaves.

Harvesting the grain

As part of their wages, they received bacon and bread. I remember Cousin Jozsi in front of the coach shed that afternoon, weighing the white, salted bacon. One by one the peasants received their portion. As it got dark, the families sat down in small groups, and roasted slices of bacon on sticks over little fires. In the background the sky, sprinkled with a myriad of tiny stars, seemed blacker than usual because of the contrast with the flickering bright flames. The absorbed faces of the people colored red by the flames, their outstretched hands holding those sticks to the fire, suggested some old pagan ritual. Nature painting with black, red, yellow, and some sprinkles of silver created an unforgettable picture.

Roasting bacon

"Lunch is ready!" The voice of Zoli's wife brought us back to the present. After lunch we sat talking for a while. As in any gathering, the main topic was who came home and who was missing. Then it was time to go.

We decided to return by train, and had a long walk to the railroad station at the other end of the village. I didn't mind the walk as it was a pleasant day. As we were walking, Sanyi and Laycsi pointed out houses that had belonged to their family or to other Jewish families in the village. We passed the temple, which was badly in need of repair, and after another stretch, Uncle Dezső's manor, an elegant country house, nestled behind some tall pine trees.

We met some people who greeted Laycsi with, "Good afternoon, Mr. Friedman," but their eyes were on the ground. Their consciences were bothering them. They were embarrassed at having stood by and done nothing while Laycsi's family was destroyed during the war. Since the Friedmans were a prosperous family, many had profited from their misfortune. Laycsi was not ready to forgive them. "They have plenty to be ashamed of," he remarked to us bitterly.

Uncle Dezsö's Manor

Married!

Summer passed, then fall went by. I was still waiting for members of my family to come home. No one else returned. I had to resign myself to the fact that all that was left of my family was my sister and my two brothers.

One day late in the fall, I received a telegram from Laci Vamos's mother: "Come immediately. Laci is home and sick." After the liberation of Budapest, Mrs. Vamos and her daughter Duci returned to Nagyvarad (Oradea). Duci and I had kept up a correspondence. Sanyi still had not asked me to marry him. I decided that I would not wait any longer. That afternoon I went to his apartment and I asked him flatly, "Will you marry me? If not I'll leave tomorrow for Nagyvarad."

He was surprised and said slowly, "I am not ready to get married. I can't support a family."

I left speechless. I couldn't sleep all night, I was so disappointed and hurt. The next day I was packing when Sanyi came in. "Don't go," he said. "I love you. We will manage somehow. I'll marry you." Then he embraced me. He gave me jewelry of his mother's that he had found hidden in the cellar of their house. We were married on December 7, 1945.

I moved to an apartment that Sanyi had rented on Arpad Street. Sanyi had been living with two cousins: Feri Brown, the son of his father's older sister, and Imre Rothman, the son Sanyi's father's younger sister. Feri was twelve years older and Imre two years younger than Sanyi. Both cousins continued to live with us.

Sanyi had opened a wholesale grocery and liquor store with two friends. It was a good partnership. They got along well and made good money. But Feri persuaded Sanyi to buy out his partners, saying, "Why should you have strangers as partners? The two of us can manage the store." Older and more experienced than Sanyi, who trusted him, he soon became the sole owner of the store. After that we tried to make a go of a small retail store, but it didn't take off, and at the end of 1947, when the communist regime took over the government of the country, we were forced to close down. All private holdings—real estate, fields, factories, stores—were nationalized. As a result, small retail stores had no place from which to buy merchandise to restock. Because it was more difficult to remove people from their lands than from a business, many people who owned lands were pronounced *kulaks* and put into internment camps. Sanyi's cousins Jozsi and Zoli were interned in one such camp.

In May of 1946, Imre managed to emigrate to Israel with the first Youth Aliah. In January 1946, Feri got married. He and his wife had a little girl the same year. Using connections and bribes, Feri and his family succeeded in obtaining passports in the fall of 1947 and left for Israel. By then Sanyi and I were also trying to leave Romania but we didn't have the money or the connections.

The House Where Sanyi Was Born

Our apartment house at 11 Arpad Street had a big backyard and behind the backyard a huge garden with vegetable plots and fruit trees. In May 1946 we went down to the garden and spread a blanket under an old walnut tree. We were in love. I was expecting my first child. The cherry trees were in bloom. The air was filled with the scent of spring and the buzzing of bees. A soft wind tickled our skin. We had been half-aware of the sound of a hammer hitting an anvil, when the characteristic odor of burning hoof hit our noses. Sanyi suddenly sat up excitedly, pointed to a two-story building behind the fence of our garden and said, "Look, that is the house I was born in! I spent my childhood there."

"Tell me about your childhood," I said. Sanyi lay back in my lap, looked into the blue sky and started to reminisce.

Ours was the last apartment on the second floor. The building was in the back of a blacksmith shop, on Hunyadi Street. From the deck in front of the apartment I could see into the shop. In the far corner, the smith's apprentice worked the bellows, keeping the coals hot. Sparks flew all over as the blacksmith turned the iron about to be forged on the red-hot coals. When the iron was hot enough, the smith put it on the anvil. He turned the iron with long tweezers-like pliers that he held in one hand, while with his other hand he clinked away at the anvil with a small hammer, showing his helper where to strike the iron with his big forging hammer. "Chinn, chinn, chinn"—the smith forms the hot iron with his small hammer. "Clink" on the anvil—one blow from the smith. "Plang"—a blow with the big forging hammer. Clink, clink. Plang, plang. The smith and his helper chatted in the midst of the fireworks started by the hammering.

Sitting on my little stool I could watch the shoeing of horses and oxen. First one man would clean the animal's hooves with a big rasp while another man held the animal's leg. I always wondered why the men weren't afraid of the horse kicking or biting them. When the hooves were clean, they put the red-hot horseshoe on the hoof to see how it fit. A cloud of bad-smelling smoke spread all over. They then gave the horseshoe a few more blows on the anvil and then they'd dip the hot shoe in a barrel of water, and nail it to the hoof with funny, nearly square nails. Later, when I was older, I would sometimes find a horseshoe nail and trade it at the cheder for four or five big buttons.

The blacksmith shop

Every so often the coal man would come to the blacksmith's. He came in a huge covered wagon drawn by two little mountain ponies. One of the ponies had a tiny foal that followed closely behind his mother. The little foal had a collar with bells on his neck. The man usually had with him his son, a little boy about ten or twelve years old. They both wore typical linen Romanian clothes. Once white, their clothes were now black from the coal. Both were sweating as they unloaded the sacks of wood coal, which they made somewhere in the forests of the mountains where they lived.

The coal dust mixed with the sweat of their faces, painting them black all over, except for their pink mouths and their shining eyes. I always wondered what his Mamma did to the boy before putting him to bed. There would have been no end to the scrubbing and soaking I would have received.

My mother was fourteen years younger than my father. Unlike most marriages in those days, theirs was not arranged by a matchmaker. In the summer of 1918, almost at the end of World War I, my father came home on furlough from the front and met my mother at a dance party. She was a beautiful, slender eighteen year old, the dance queen of the party, he a handsome, decorated sergeant. They fell in love. They married after the war ended and moved to Szatmar, where my father opened a textile yardage and haberdashery store with a partner. I was born on November 11, 1923.

Some fragments of my early childhood I remember vividly. My oldest memory is sitting on Zaydi's knees: I see in my mind's eye a very old, tall, thin man with a long white beard, looking at me with his piercing blue eyes, holding in his mouth a cherry wood pipe that came all the way down to his waist. In my mental picture Zaydi is always smoking a long pipe, and the picture is saturated with the smell of sharp tobacco smoke.

Another vivid memory is of my first day in cheder. I was about three years old. My father walked me to the cheder holding my hand and left me there. I sat next to the rabbi, a short fat man with a faded reddish beard. He was sitting at the head of a long table in a large armchair of woven straw like the one in the painting "Van Gogh Chair."

*On both sides of the table children my age and a little older sat on long benches, with old, worn books in front of them and read in loud chorus the Alef-Bait: "*kometz alef oo, kometz bait boo,….*" Occasionally if the choir's volume fell or the rhythm slowed the Rebbe would hit the table with his bamboo stick. It sounded like thunder. Then he joined the choir with his deep voice: "*Kometz gimmel goo, kometz daled doo….*" My heart*

The cheder

would sink and I would tremble inside. The Rebbe smiled at me and tried to encourage me. But it didn't help. For one thing, he called me "Smuel-Mayer." Until then I had been "Sanyi" or "Sanyika." The Rebbe let me sit and watch for a few days. Then he put me on his lap and showed me on a big chart, "Smuel-Mayer," he said, "see, here is an *Alef*—a slanted bar with two little pitchers, one on top, the other below it." I was looking, but not at the *Alef*. Instead, I was looking at the little hand at the end of his pointer. "How tiny a finger, how perfect! Who could have made that?" I wondered.

Every morning Esther, the cashier from my father's store, would take me to the store. From there, her brother Pista, the apprentice, a big boy of about thirteen, would walk with me to the cheder. There was a chilly feeling in my chest every time we arrived. I was a quiet and shy child. Even when I was older, my heart would shudder at the idea of meeting a stranger. At noon,

Pista would pick me up and take me back to the store where I would stay until the store closed for lunch. Then my father would take me home.

When I got older, I walked from the cheder to the store alone. I had to cross the town square. There used to be a marketplace in the town square where the central park is. Every morning the peasants from the surrounding villages would sell their fresh produce there. On market days the city's craftsman would also display their merchandise. Each vendor made a tent. The tents were arranged in rows, a row for the boot-makers, one for the tailors, another for the cabinet and furniture makers, one for sheet-metal, one for every craft. I used to wander between the rows of tents admiring the merchandise, watching the people, selling and buying. Then with some friends I would turn the big wheel of the water pump which used to be across from the Panonia Hotel. We all got soaking wet before we left.

My father's store sold yardage, haberdashery, and toys. I loved it there. I used to watch my father and his partner fix the shop window. What marvelous shapes they would create! How I wished to have one of those little hammers used for hammering in pins! And how proud I was when people stopped and admired the window! But the real fun was the stock room, in the back of the shop. Bales of textile fabrics were stored in a pleasant semi-darkness. I could climb piles of soft woolen shawls and hide in them. There were empty boxes I could build houses and forts from. Sometimes, if I promised to be very careful, father allowed me to play with some of the toys that were for sale. I remember a little wagon with red wheels drawn by two little oxen mounted on a platform with tiny cams that moved the oxen's legs. I loaded the wagon with tiny boxes, tied a string to the yoke, and pulled it.

I loved to play all alone in the stock room. Sometimes I would hear my father's voice: "Go see what that child's doing." Then quickly, I would put back the things I wasn't supposed to touch before my cousin Feri got there. Feri, the son of my father's older sister, was a junior salesman. He had already finished the apprentice school. Now, with a pair of shiny scissors and pencils in the cigar pocket of his jacket he put on the air of a grownup. He was sixteen or seventeen and insisted that Pista, the apprentice, who was younger but a lot bigger and stronger than him (later he became a professional soccer player) call him "Mr." Feri.

On Wednesdays the store didn't close for lunch. Wednesdays were market days and instead of going home, my mother used to bring our lunch to the store. Everybody would eat in the stock room, and I didn't have to behave at the table. Wednesdays were even better if the store was busy, and Mommy stayed on to help. She bundled me into something warm and put me down for a nap. As soon she left I crawled out and settled into a long period of undisturbed playing. As I got older, my favorite plaything was a small wooden toolbox filled with all kinds of nails that came from the wooden cases and crates in which the merchandise arrived. I straightened the nails and tried to nail together the thin wood frames left over from the emptied yardage pieces. I hit my fingers many times. It hurt enough to bring tears to my eyes, but I never cried out loud. I treasured my undisturbed privacy too much to exchange it for sympathy

Fridays were busy days in our house, cooking and preparing for Shabbat. Thursday evening Mommy would prepare the dough for chala, bread, and pastries. Then Friday morning the servant girl would knead the dough for the bread. Later, while I was sitting on the bed to stay out of the way, she would scrub the floor and Mommy would twist the chala and bake the cheese Danish and the chocolate coffee cake. The cheese Danish were called delkelis. There has been nothing like them since. Daddy came home early on Fridays, and we men went to the temple. I liked to walk holding Daddy's hand. When we returned home, the Shabbat candles were lit, two chalas were waiting at Daddy's place on the table, the Kiddish cup was filled with sweet wine, the table was set, and Mommy was dressed up nicely. There was an air of happiness in the whole room as Daddy entered with a cheerful, "Good Shabbos, Good Shabbos" and embraced Mommy.

They greeted each other like they hadn't seen each other for ages. Then Daddy placed his handkerchief on my head, put his hand over it, and blessed me, and Mommy kissed me. I liked that. Daddy made Kiddish, took a sip, and offered the wine to me and then to Mommy. Mommy put her finger in the cup and gave my baby sister Ibi a taste. We washed our hands for the motzi, *the blessing over the bread, and ate dinner. I usually fell asleep before dinner was over. It was always so warm and pleasant.*

One Saturday morning, when I was about seven, Mommy dressed me in my new Shabbos clothes, a navy-blue sailor suit with blue stripes on its large white collar and cuffs, shiny black patent-leather shoes, white knee-socks, and a flat cap with two ribbons hanging on the side. I had reddish-blond hair and green eyes. Mommy said I looked "like something" and I was sure that was the highest praise in the world.

First thing in the morning, Daddy and I went to the temple. When we got home at noon, the Shabbos lunch was waiting— fish, soup, and cholent, compote, fruits, and goodies. After lunch Mommy and Daddy would take a short nap. While they were sleeping, I was supposed to stay outside on the terrace with the servant girl, Lemke. I remember one occasion when I was watching the blacksmith shop and Lemke was chatting with a helper from the joiner shop while keeping an eye on me. Then she told me to stay where I was, that she would be back in a minute, and went inside the shop with him. They stayed more than a minute and I got bored. Slowly I wandered down to the yard. It was a little scary—all those sweating men I didn't know and trampling horses. Nobody noticed me. I got to the back of the yard. I climbed onto the driver's seat of a flat wagon and said, "Prr!!! Go you lazy beasts," as I had heard the drivers say to their horses. That finished, I climbed onto a peasant wagon. One of its front wheels was off the axle. I tried to lift the axle but it was too heavy. I couldn't move it. My hands got black and greasy. I cleaned them on the grass. Then I wiped them on my trousers. Just then I noticed a coach with black leather seats and shade cover. I climbed in the back seat, pretended to tell the address to the coachman and leaned back. Then I climbed in the driver's seat. I was the squire with six white horses. "Gyu you, Kesely! Faster, faster." It got very hot. Sweating, I wandered into the open coal shed and looked around. I saw sacks of coal and a big shovel. I picked up the shovel and tried to gather the loose coal. The cloud of dust made me sneeze. I wiped the sweat off my face with my hand, then I climbed on top of the coal sacks to rest. I had almost fallen asleep when I heard Mommy calling, "Sanyi, Sanyi, where are you? It's time to go to grandma's house."

"Coming, Mommy," I replied.

When she saw me she exclaimed, "Got in himmel, what happened to you?" She lifted me up to the mirror so I could see myself. I looked and also wondered what had happened. That wasn't me in the mirror; it was the coal man's little boy, or perhaps a little devil.

Every weekend, on Saturday or Sunday afternoon, we walked to grandma's house. Father's mother lived on the outskirts of the city. The walk took well over an hour. As we left our street, we turned onto Rakolci Street which, instead of cobblestones like our street had, was paved with little, square bricks. When the firemen passed on their sprinkler wagon, the street became shiny and smelled so fresh.

In the center of the street were the tracks for the "Choo-choo" train, which people called the "coffee grinder." It passed right through the city, stopping at the town square in front of the big Panonia Hotel. From there it went through Vardomb (Fortress Hill) Street, across the bridge, and left the city.

On weekdays the streets were busy. There were lots of people on the sidewalk. Horse-drawn carriages and large and small flat wagons loaded with all kinds of things filled the road. It was noisy and colorful. Occasionally, when one of the few auto-cars or the train belching smoke and steam passed by, the horse drivers had to hold the reins tight.

On weekends the streets were quiet and the stores were closed.

As we got closer to the town square, the display windows got bigger and more colorful. When we got to Daddy's store, we always stopped to look at the window. Daddy's store was in a long building with many other stores. First there was a delicatessen with salamis, fish, cheeses, and wine bottles in the window. Then came a china store, with plates and porcelain figurines that Mommy liked to look at. Then came Daddy's store. To me his store was the nicest of them all. At the next corner, there was a candy store. How I wished my Daddy owned that store!

As we got to the county courthouse, a huge building with heavy steel bars on the basement windows, I imagined the dangerous criminals who were locked in the dark cellars, and I was afraid. "What if a murderer escaped just as we were walking by?" I asked myself. Then I thought, "My Daddy is very strong, he could surely overcome even the biggest criminal." I grabbed my Daddy's hand and held it tight. Sometimes we would turn into the street with the theater. The theater had a round front, and on both sides, the entry stairs had a low wall you could climb and walk on. The main attraction of this route was the fact that at the corner of the promenade, under the electric clock, stood Mr. Turk, the ice cream vendor with the best ice cream in the world. (I wonder if Mr. Turk really was Turkish. He must have been because he talked with an accent unlike that of anybody else I knew.)

We would walk to the Panonia Hotel and Restaurant. In the summer people sat at little garden tables under umbrellas in front of the restaurant. The busboys continuously sprinkled water on the hot asphalt to make the sweating customers more comfortable.

At the alley by the hotel we went back to Rakolci Street. From the alley we could see the firemen's watchtower. It looked like a factory's chimney, only taller. Through the cracks and holes of the plank fence, I could see the fire pumps lined up in an open shed. Occasionally I would see a fireman with his shiny brass hat fetching some horses to harness to a fire wagon. They had the nicest and fastest horses in town. When I finished the ice cream cone I bought from Mr. Turk, I helped Mommy push my little sister's baby carriage. We still had a long walk to grandma's house; usually we took a rest in the small park in front of the big city hospital.

Early Years under Communism

Sanyi and I lived in the apartment on Arpad Street for eighteen years. Both our children were born there—Ibi on December 2, 1946, and Joseph on March 23, 1953. We named Ibi after Sanyi's sister, Joseph after Sanyi's father.

My sister Ibi married David (Dezső) Steinberger, a well-known tailor, in March 1946. An artist in his trade, he later founded Mondiala, one of the largest state-owned clothing factories in Romania, and, with about three thousand workers, one of the largest employers in town. Dezső was the fashion designer. Dezső and Ibi, had two children Laci and Aniko, each six months younger than my children.

Ibi, Dezső, Sanyi, and I became each other's family. Having children the same age, we spent a lot of time together.

When the communist regime took over, everything became state-owned and everybody became a salaried employee of the state. The best-paying jobs were given to Communist Party members. The qualification of the boss was his party membership. Knowledge and experience did not count.

Since neither Alex nor I were party members, it took a while until we got jobs. First Sanyi was offered a job at a transport and hauling company. He said he did not know anything about transporting, and he was told, "You don't have to know anything. You just have to inform us what's going on there." He refused the job, but many did not refuse similar jobs. To impose communist rule, almost everybody had been approached to inform on whether neighbors and co-workers were disloyal to the new regime. Having refused this offer, he couldn't find another job. And then things got worse.

In late summer of 1948, Sanyi decided to look up a friend, one of three former partners of his who had moved to Timisoara. He was hoping for help in finding a job. As Sanyi was standing in line for a train ticket, an acquaintance of his asked him where was he going. Sanyi told him he was going to Timisoara. The acquaintance offered to pay half of the train fair if Sanyi would take a small package to someone in that city. This wasn't an unusual request because the mail was slow and unreliable. Sanyi agreed, delivered the package, and we forgot all about it.

Nothing panned out in Timisoara. Later, with great difficulty, Sanyi was able to get a job as a salesman at the state grocery store in Szatmar. The salary was very small and the work thankless. For a while there was only one grocery store in the entire city of sixty thousand people. People had to stand in line for everything, and even the most basic staples ran out before the end of the line was served. Later the state opened a few more stores, but the lines had become a fixture of daily life because there was a shortage of most essentials. We stood in line for bread at the bread store; for sugar, oil, rice, and soap at the grocery store; for milk, butter, and cheese at the milk store. Once in a blue moon there was meat and then there were endless lines at the butcher's. Most of the time the stores were empty. It was not unusual for people to queue up at midnight just to be sure to have an opportunity to buy something when the store opened at eight o'clock. It was a full-time job just to stay in line for food, and the same was true for clothing. Even many years after the war, lines were part of everyday life.

Sanyi had been working at the state grocery for almost a year when one morning two men from the Securitate (State Security Police) demanded to search our home. We didn't know what they wanted and they didn't tell us what they were looking for. They didn't find anything, but they arrested Sanyi and took him to the Department of State Security. We still had no idea what he was accused of. I asked my brother-in-law Dezső, who I knew was a friend of the chief of the Securitate, to try to find out what Sanyi was accused of. The chief told him it was not his case, and all he knew was that the Securitate in Nagyvarad requested that Sanyi be sent there as part of an investigation of a smuggling ring which encompassed several cities. The ring smuggled people over the border to the West and brought back black market goods—especially nylon stockings, silk shawls, penicillin, and wristwatches. The package Sanyi had delivered to Timisoara contained smuggled goods. The person who had received the package was arrested, and under interrogation he had implicated Sanyi.

Sanyi tried in vain to tell the police that he had nothing to do with the whole thing. For two weeks he was interrogated, beaten, and tortured every night. In the first few weeks, he was in a cell with other political detainees—a young priest, a teacher, and others accused of being enemies of the state. Later he was moved to solitary confinement. He was kept in a dark, damp, cold, four-by-six-foot cell. He had no pillow or blanket. He slept on the bare planks of a wooden bed. Once a day he was given a cup of bean or cabbage soup, without the beans or cabbage. Those were picked out by the guards.

Once a month relatives were allowed to bring prisoners food and a change of clothing. Every month, I traveled from Szatmar to Nagyvarad, carrying my baby Ibike. He never received the food I brought for him, but I didn't know that until later. When I received his dirty clothes, I knew that he was still alive.

Trying to obtain his release, I went to the house of the chief investigator, but I wasn't able to get in. With my baby in my arms, I followed him and his cronies to a restaurant. I went in after them to plead that my husband was innocent. They laughed and made fun of me.

After eight months, a trial was scheduled and, in the middle of the night, the accused were transferred to the court's penitentiary. Some of them were carried on stretchers because, weak from hunger and beatings, they couldn't walk. A few days after their transfer I was allowed a short visit. When I saw Sanyi I was thrilled because I thought he had gained weight. I didn't know that he looked heavier because he was swollen from hunger. Before the trial started Sanyi was taken back to the Securitate, where they gave him back his personal belongings and told him to go home. They had known for months that he was not part of the ring and yet they had not released him. Walking towards the train station, Sanyi kept looking over his shoulders. He thought they were playing some kind of game with him.

In the fall of 1949, one of Sanyi's former partners became the commercial supervisor of the distribution center for the county's cooperatives, and he offered Sanyi a job. The stores in all the villages of the county received all their merchandise from this distribution center. As in all other institutions, the chiefs of the departments had to be party members. But to run such a huge operation, people with commercial experience were needed. The solution hit upon was to have two people in every position—one who knew about running a business and his boss, a member of the Party. The same system was at work all over the country.

Sanyi's friend had arranged Sanyi's transfer to the book department. The job paid a little more than the grocery store and it wasn't so strenuous. Sanyi's boss was Tovarasul Dumitru Pop. Between the two of them they were in charge of the stationery and book department. Pop was the boss with the big salary because he was a party member, and Sanyi did the work. Pop had been transferred there because he had been demoted. He had thought that his wife had been unfaithful to him and had tried to commit suicide. His wife, Ethel, was also a party activist. She was the secretary of the regional Communist Women's Organization. They both came from a small mining town, where before they become Communist Party members, he was a mechanic and she was a helper in the local pub.

It was the end of summer and schools were reopening. The stationery and book department was responsible for the distribution of the school books and supplies for all the schools in the villages of the whole county. Pop and his wife invited us to their home. Pop told us that he couldn't sleep nights because he was sure that he'd end up in jail. All those bales of merchandise, a tremendous number of packages of books—he just didn't know what to do with them. He'd mixed up everything so badly that supplies were missing, and frightened, he had bought what was necessary to cover the shortages at a local retail store with his own money. Both he and his wife were very grateful that Sanyi took over running of the department.

After a year or so Pop got another job and his wife was promoted to president of the clothing factory where my brother-in-law was the fashion designer. She brought Sanyi to the factory and put him in charge of maintenance and new construction of the factory's buildings. This was a better-paying job, but still we both had to struggle to make ends meet. I took a job, sewing in the lingerie department of the factory.

In the beginning the factory did not have a day-care center for the employees' children. We both left for work in the morning while Ibike, our three year old, was still asleep in her bed. We left her food on a plate, milk in a cup, a slice of bread spread with marmalade, and an empty potty next to her bed. We returned home at three or three-thirty to find the cup and plate empty and the potty full. By the time she was four, the factory had a child-care center, so we were able to take her with us every morning and pick her up after work.

One early morning in the spring, we could not find Ibike when we got up. We looked everywhere—inside the apartment, at the neighbors, in the garden, in the park across the street. There was no trace of her. I was worried sick. She had just disappeared. On a hunch, Sanyi jumped on his bicycle to check if by chance she had managed to go to the day-care center. And there she was, sitting at a long table with the other children, eating breakfast. Both her cheeks and her mouth were smudged with jam. Her long, curly hair was a terrific, uncombed mess, and her left shoe was on her right foot. But, as always, she was smiling happily. She had wakened early and got herself dressed. The sun had been out—days were getting longer. We were still asleep in the other room, and all was quiet. She thought that we had left without her. She had heard our next-door neighbors getting ready to leave, and, not realizing that they left for work earlier than we did, she had told the neighbors that we had forgotten to take her. She had asked if she could go to the day-care center with them and they had taken her.

No matter how we tried to stretch our money, our salaries were never enough. One winter I was able to buy Ibike a pair of thick gray stockings. I would wash them every night, and she wore them again the next day. To make sure they would dry, I laid them on the fireplace overnight. The fireplace was a tall, rectangular box about eight feet high and made of tiles. A shelf jutted out from it. The fire was made in the base of the box. The tiles absorbed the heat and then released it slowly, heating the room. One night, I must have put the stockings on the shelf earlier than usual because in the morning they were singed. A brown line ran down them. When Ibike came home from the day-care center, she said that the other kids made fun of her—the burn mark was poop, they said. We never had enough money to replace the stockings that winter.

We got paid twice a month. There was never enough to

last until the next payday. Every two weeks, I borrowed and repaid our neighbors, Dr. Cira and his wife, Erzsike, who were about 20 years older than Sanyi and I. He had been the mayor of the town before the war and owned property in the country. They were not as poverty stricken as we were. They never said no, but Erzsike did everything slowly and deliberately, while I was always fast and in a hurry. Dr. Cira saw that I found it humiliating to have to wait for her to lend me the money, and he would tell her in the polite second-person form of address that they used with each other, "Please, be so kind as to give it to her already." Often they told us that our children were so beautiful we should have a dozen. I was flattered, but I would think of how much I wished my mother were alive to see my children.

Mrs. Cira taught me how to cook. When I borrowed small amounts of sugar or lard, she told me to take it myself. She made sure not to look so that I could take a little extra if I needed it. If she heard my children cry, she would check up on what was happening, asking in her slow, polite way, "What are you doing to them? You are not skinning them, are you?" She knew I wasn't hurting them. It was her way of being there for me. She and Ibike became great friends. Ibike loved to camp out at her house.

Our Own Business

In the middle 1950s the government relaxed economic restrictions and issued some private business licenses for small enterprises. The owner, working himself, could sell his products at marketplaces and fairs. A second cousin, Shaje Brecher, taking advantage of the new freedom, sold peasant garments at the fairs. The garments were made by people who worked for him in their homes. I asked him to give me some work. I told him how we struggled to live on our salary. We had spent winters eating nothing but potatoes. He said,

"You can do better than this. Come to my booth tomorrow, and I'll show you something." Next day at his booth in the marketplace, he showed me a woman selling aprons for peasant women and shirts for men. "This is what you should do," he told me.

Sanyi and I took out a permit to sell goods privately, and Shaje showed me where to buy factory seconds and damaged and remnant material at very low prices. I did the sewing and Sanyi the cutting and pressing. I had quit my job, but Sanyi still held on to his. About a week later, early in the morning on a Tuesday, I went with Shaje and some other merchants to the fair at a nearby town. By the time I closed my booth in the evening, I had sold everything. I made more money that one day than in a whole month of our combined salaries.

Sanyi quit his job. I cut the material, he went to the fairs, and we had five or six women sewing for us in their homes. By this time, Dr. Cira had died and Mrs. Cira, who had been reduced to poverty, was also working for us, sewing. It wasn't an easy way to make a living, but we were motivated by the financial success. Everyday we went to weekly market days, monthly fairs, or big regional fairs. The further the fair was from a big city or railroad, the better the business. Naturally, distant fairs were also more strenuous. At least two or three times a month, we left for a fair as early as three or four o'clock in the morning. We traveled by horse-drawn carriages, or if we were lucky, on the back of an open truck, sitting on top of whatever it was carrying. We stayed at the fair in winter in freezing cold and in summer in scorching heat till five or six o'clock in the afternoon. The trip home was another three or four hours of travel.

For a couple of years we did very well. At home, a peasant servant girl cooked and watched the children. We could buy everything we needed or wanted, if not in the state stores, then certainly on the black market. We will always feel grateful to Shaje Brecher for his advice and help.

For a time, Hebrew schools, which the communist regime had closed down, were permitted to reopen. We sent our son Joska every day after public school. He was a very serious child who thought things over on his own. One afternoon he met my brother-in-law Dezsö on his way to Hebrew school. Dezsö asked Joska if he liked to go there. Joska thought about it and then replied, "I like to come home from there." We laughed hard when Dezsö told us about it. Joska was quite a character throughout his childhood. He noticed that when he cried I tried to comfort him. As he got older, when he wanted my attention, he would announce, "Mom, I will cry." He thought it was enough to warn me without going through all the effort of crying.

By 1955, we were doing so well that we decided to take a family vacation. For the first time since the war, it was possible to obtain a passport to go to Hungary. Sanyi and I and our two kids went to Budapest for two weeks to visit my brother and his family. One of the first things we did was to look up Mr. Klemencsics to thank him for all that he had done for me. He was happy to see me and my family. He would not accept praise. He said, "I didn't do much. Every decent person would have done that much and maybe should have done more." Maybe he was right. But there were few people decent or courageous enough to do anything. We tried to locate Maria Kirtag but had no success.

A year later, in October 1956, we again obtained a passport to visit my brother. Because there wasn't enough room for us at my brother's two-bedroom apartment, we rented the house-attendant's bedroom. We stayed all day with my brother's family, and we went next door to sleep. We arrived a few days before the Hungarian Revolution erupted. It wasn't totally unexpected. We could feel a mood of passion and excitement in the air. And in the train and on the trams, people talked openly about things they wouldn't have dared to whisper about in Romania.

Then the revolution exploded in its full fury. In a brief fight the revolutionaries took over the radio station, the police stations, and the Hungarian military barracks. The soldiers were told to go home. Many joined the revolutionaries. In a surprise attack the revolutionaries drove the occupying Soviet forces from the city, burning tanks, trucks, and missile-launchers with "Molotov cocktails"—quart bottles filled with gasoline.

There was an ugly aspect to the revolution. People hunted their opponents, executing them on the spot. Many private feuds were avenged under the guise of revolutionary action. It was open season on members of the AVO (State Defense Detachment, the secret police). One could get caught in cross-fire any time, any place. To provoke a disturbance, snipers from rooftops would shoot at people standing in line for bread. Dead bodies were lying in the streets, reminiscent of the terrible days of 1945. There were no police, no authority of any kind, no way to distinguish friend from foe.

Like all people in Budapest, my brother didn't have a pantry full of food. Everybody used to buy their necessities daily from the stores and the central market hall. Now, with the hall closed and the stores looted, the population was in a frenzy looking for food. The city's bakers proved to be reliable and even heroic. The bakeries worked constantly, and there were always lines outside them. The bakers sold bread straight from the oven from dawn till dusk, then worked all night to prepare and bake next day's bread.

In spite of the danger of being on the streets, four children and four adults had to be fed, and Sanyi and I preferred the danger to being cooped up inside. We stood in line daily for bread. We found warehouses where they were selling potatoes, vegetables, and apples. Often gunfire, from no identifiable place, drove us into entry halls or under overturned streetcars for cover. We walked everywhere because there was no public transportation. The buses and trams had been overturned by the mob in the heat of revolution.

One day while out hunting for food, we saw a commotion in front of us. We heard loud voices yelling, "He is an AVO man!" Next thing we knew the body of a man was hanging by a rope from a lamp post. I can't forget the dark blue face of that hanging man. The whole episode took less than five minutes.

The revolution ran its course quickly. The revolutionaries' calls for help from Western countries, through Radio Budapest, remained unanswered. Two weeks after leaving the city, the Russians returned. We were awakened in the middle of the night by the loud concussion of nearby canon fire. The tenants from the upstairs apartments ran downstairs in panic. All of us watched in horror the flashes of explosions that illuminated the sky in the direction of the Korut (Circular Avenue). The stillness that followed the departing roar was even more frightening than the noise. In the morning we discovered that the Russian Army had returned. In retaliation for the casualties they had suffered, they fired a canon blast at every second house on each side of the main streets on their way into Budapest.

We thought that the unfolding events might bring us an opportunity to escape to the West. We went to the Israeli Consulate to ask if they could help us leave for Israel. The consul was in Vienna. Having left a few days before the revolution erupted, he was unable to return. We were told to leave our passports, return in two or three days, and they would see what could be done. When we went back the consul still had not been able to return. We were told to try again later and our passports were returned to us. Disappointed, we walked back home. On the way, finding an apple vendor, we bought as many as he would sell us. Suddenly machine gun fire made us and everybody else in the street run for cover. Sanyi and I, each holding one handle of the shopping bag with the apples, ran into the entry hall of a building. As we entered a bullet broke a button on my winter coat.

The tension from eight people locked up for weeks in a two-room apartment became intolerable. Full of regret, we gave up hope of escape and we arranged our return to Romania at the Romanian Legation. Talking to us through the wrought iron fence surrounding the compound, a civilian added our names to a list. Early next day we came back with our children. Someone checked our passports against the names on the list and we embarked on a waiting bus with a large Romanian flag on the front.

When everybody was seated, the man with the list got in next to the driver and we left. As the bus drove through the city we could see evidence of the fighting—buildings in ruins, abandoned tanks and armored cars everywhere. We saw skeletons on top of tank hulks or in the hatches. They were what was left of soldiers who had been trapped in the burning tanks.

At one point armed civilians with the Hungarian National tricolor armbands stopped the bus. The man with the list talked to their leader, who walked through the bus briefly looking at the people and then let the bus proceed. A short while after we left the city, Russian soldiers, who had vacated the city but kept it surrounded tightly, stopped the bus. Again the man with the list talked to the officer in charge, and we continued our journey. The bus took us to the border. There everybody got back their passports, and continued their trip home by train.

At home we had to return our passports to the Securitate. We were told not to talk to anyone about the events in Budapest. For a long time we could feel that we were kept under surveillance. Four or five weeks later, when we learned from the BBC and Radio Free Europe that people were escaping by the tens of thousands to Austria, we were literally sick. When we were there a month earlier, even the thought of daring to do so was preposterous. "Going away, where? Why? America and her allies will be here soon," everyone kept telling us. And when it became clear that the West was not coming, people said, "Going away? The corpses are six deep at the borders." So we returned to Romania. We left at my brother's a large amount of Hungarian money we had made selling goods we brought from Romania that were hard to find in Budapest—coffee beans, pepper, flannel fabrics. My brother and his family used the money to arrange to leave Hungary. They emigrated to the United States.

A few of the merchants at the fair were selling silk-screened shawls and kerchiefs for the village women. That gave Sanyi the idea to make silk-screened handkerchiefs for children. He drew cartoons illustrating well-known children's stories. He paid someone to teach him to make the silk-screens, mix the paint, and do the printing. We made sample pieces.

A friend of ours, the state grocery store's executive director, presented the collection to the state distribution center's buyer, who gave us a trial order. The cooperative where we worked bought the fabric and we delivered the first order. The retail price of every item was set by the central office. It usually consisted of the cost of raw material plus labor and the profit allotted to the producers. The labor was computed from the time needed for each phase by a worker qualified to do that phase. Each qualified skill had an associated established wage. Instead of this system, with the consent of the cooperative's leaders—who got their share—we calculated backwards. Starting from the established retail price for a comparable product, we deducted the cost of raw material and the cooperative's profit and we set aside the rest for labor. Then we divided the total labor into phases, assigning the prescribed wages to each phase.

Sanyi and I accomplished all the phases ourselves, except

for the hemming. We made and maintained the silk screens, mixed the paints, printed the designs, and packaged the finished product. In addition, we were responsible for managing the whole operation. Although we did almost all the work, it just didn't look good on paper that our earnings were so much higher than that of the others. The solution came from the officials who also needed to justify their own high income. When the state buyer saw that the article was selling, he ordered a larger quantity, on the condition that we have his and my friend's wife engaged as workers. They did not want to work, and we didn't really pay them. They wanted relatives to be on the payroll to justify their income and to receive vacation tickets and health benefits. It was a convenient solution for everyone.

We made much more money than we possibly could spend without attracting attention. It was tempting to try, like so many did, to convert our money into reliable, portable assets by buying dollars or diamonds on the black market, and then wait for the chance to smuggle them out of Romania. We were lucky we didn't do so. Most of those who did were caught and sentenced to many years of hard labor.

Emigration to Israel or the West went on at a slow pace. We heard that Israel was paying money to Romania for each emigrant. Except for special cases, the choice of the persons allowed to emigrate to Israel was that of the Romanian bureaucracy. It was like a lottery. A few from one city, a few from another city were given permission. Some who filed their application much later got their exit visas before the ones who filed years earlier. When someone who received a passport was suspected of possessing dollars, he was taken to the Securitate and tortured to tell not only where he kept his "possession," but also from whom he bought it.

It was modern torture—no beatings that left marks. Instead the victim was made to stand in a windowless dark room with a very strong light aimed at him. He was given no food or water until he collapsed or admitted having dollars. Some were kept for days while the interrogators, who were changed every four hours, continually threatened to revoke their passports if they didn't confess. After the victim had fainted several times the policemen believed that he really did not possess dollars, diamonds, or gold coins. But then they tried to persuade him to tell who in his opinion might have some.

We were always very careful not to attract attention by excessive spending, and never had any connection with those selling dollars or other illegal goods in the black market. And we let it be known that if we had extra money when we got our passports, we would give it to my sister. A very good friend, who had warned us not to buy any illegal valuables, had told us that if he got his passport before us he would tell us of a way to get our money out of the country. The idea was simple and it worked. Commercial suitcases were reinforced by wooden frames which were about five centimeters wide and one centimeter thick. The handle, the hinges, and locks were mounted to these frames. Paper covered the frames and the cardboard sides. By wetting the paper lining Sanyi was able to peel the paper off the frames. Then he carefully pulled out the decorative nails holding the hinges and locks, and removed the frames. With a sharp chisel he carved a deep groove in the bottom of the frames which faced the cardboard sides. We folded the paper money, and pressed it with a hot iron, to fit it into the groove. We only used the largest denomination. After putting the money in the frames—a delicate task since the frames were now paper thin—Sanyi reinstalled everything, painstakingly making sure to put back every nail as it was before, and then he glued back the paper lining. The stamp of verification, applied at the factory to the lining on both the top and the bottom of the suitcase, was left untouched on both. Our money, ironed and folded, made it to the West before us.

Unfortunately, years later when we received it its value had diminished considerably.

We Leave Romania

Finally, in the middle of November 1964, our lucky number was drawn and we received our passports. We sold everything that we had in the house—beautiful handmade furniture, piano, Persian rugs—for bargain prices because everyone knew that we had to get rid of them quickly. To avoid suspicion, we made sure to spend the money conspicuously, buying new things. We were allowed to take with us 70 kilos for an adult and 35 kilos for a child, but nothing valuable. Knowing that when we got out we would have money waiting for us made it easier to part with our belongings. When we finally did get to customs, we had to fight to keep the few possessions that we had packed.

The morning of our last day at home, we packed our personal belongings and Sanyi took down the *Mezuzah* from the door post. We looked back at the empty apartment, and held each other tightly. Sanyi was forty-one years old and I was thirty-nine. We were both full of hope and fear but ready to face the unknown challenges ahead of us. Standing there and holding on to each other we promised that no matter what happened we would never blame one another. In the afternoon of the 31st of December 1964, we left Szatmar, the place we were born, grew up, returned to after the war, the place where our children were born.

We embarked on the train for Bucharest, accompanied by my sister. For the first time since the war, my sister and I were parting without knowing if we might ever see each other again.

The next night we slept on the floor at the house of a friend of a friend in Bucharest. Hotels weren't allowed to rent rooms for people emigrating. On the morning of January 2, 1965, at the International Airport we said a teary goodbye to my sister.

Finally, after a long time, surrounded by armed security officers, we boarded a Soviet-made airplane leaving for Naples. Every passenger on the airplane was leaving Romania for good. On the five-hour flight, we all sat quietly in our seats, talking only in whispers. It was common knowledge that the flight crew were all members of the secret police. The stewardesses offered us sweet wine. Everyone drank it obediently. Mentally, we were still in Romania, and if the authorities thought we should drink sweet wine on the airplane, we had no objections.

The plane landed in a remote area of the Naples airport. In the morning in Romania it had been freezing. When we arrived in Italy in the afternoon, we were greeted by pleasant, spring-like weather. We were met by representatives of the State of Israel who took our passports and loaded us onto two busses. In the bus we peeled off our warm winter coats and sat quietly looking out the window, trying to keep at bay thoughts of an uncertain future. On a sidestreet, we saw lines with drying clothes stretched from one side of the narrow street to the other side. People were carrying on loud conversations with neighbors. A basket dangling from a rope was pulled up from street level. The whole scene was so tranquil, so normal, and yet so different from Romania that suddenly, for the first time since we left, everybody burst out in laughter. Finally we all knew that we had really left Romania behind.

My brother Tibi from Israel met us in Rome. We paid for his fare to visit our sister in Romania. On the way back, he stopped in Budapest and picked up three of our money-lined suitcases that we had left behind. When all of our money was finally in hand, Sanyi and Ibike went to a money exchange office to convert the Romanian money to U.S. dollars. Ibike, who spoke more Italian than Sanyi, asked if they would exchange Romanian money and at what rate. The broker quoted an exchange rate. Ibike translated it to Sanyi. Sanyi knew that it was a very unfavorable rate, and told her to ask whether the exchange rate would be higher for a larger amount. The broker, checking his papers, offered a slightly more favorable rate if the money was in large denominations and if they had more than a thousand lei. "What if it is much more than a thousand?" Ibike asked. "How much more?" the broker asked. Ibike told him. Trying unsuccessfully to hide his surprise, the broker said he had to make some phone calls. Sanyi, who was sure he was calling the police, became very worried. In Romania, buying or owning U.S. dollars, "owning *valuta*," was an offense punished by jail and torture. A few minutes later, the broker came back and offered a much more favorable rate, which Sanyi accepted. "When he picked up that phone, I was so frightened I was ready to run. For a moment I was back in Romania," Sanyi told me afterwards.

Los Angeles, California

We stayed six months in Italy, until all the formalities of immigration to the U.S. were completed. On June 23, 1965, we arrived in the USA. We held alien registrations cards which would automatically become green cards in 18 months. We had new names, Alex and Rose, derived from the names— Alexandru and Rozalia—that were recorded in our Romanian emigration passports. The first few days we stayed with my brother Sandor and his family, who were overjoyed that we had succeeded in coming to Los Angeles.

Soon afterwards we rented an apartment and started working. I got a job in a sweatshop sewing sweaters for the minimum wage, $1.25 per hour. It was a very hot July, and the shop had no air-conditioning. Two fans were blowing the hot air from one side to the other, while the owner ran up and down between the two rows of sewing machines, urging us to keep up the pace. I expected him to collapse from exhaustion. Instead it was I who fainted from the heat and lack of air. After fainting several times I was fired. Each time I fainted, the work had to stop while an ambulance took me away, halting production.

Luckily, I found another job immediately through a neighbor who worked in Beverly Hills at Lucy Ann, a famous lingerie factory. I was paid $2.00 per hour working in a modern air-conditioned shop. The neighbor's husband used to drive us to work every morning. One day, as we were passing the beautiful Beverly Hills estates I told my neighbor, "You see, this is where I will live."

She looked at me and said, "You are crazy. You better come down to earth."

"You will see," I said.

Years later, visiting me in my home in Bel Air, she reminded me of our conversation. "You told me," she said.

Sanyi's first job—in a contact lens factory—paid $1.35 an hour. Joska attended junior high school, Ibike Los Angeles City College. Ibike also worked in a hospital laboratory eight hours a day on Saturdays and Sundays. She made $1.50 an hour and gave us all the money she made.

Alex and I were not disappointed or bitter over our small wages. We both knew we would be able to get better jobs when our English—which we both studied in night school—was better.

Through a friend, Sanyi got a job at a drive-in dairy, one of a chain owned and supplied by the Royal Dutch Co., a milk processing plant, for $1.65 an hour. After a few months, the plant manager asked Sanyi, "Alex! Don't you want to take over the dairy that was run by my father?" Alex told him that we had no money to buy a store.

"No, no. You don't need money," the manager said. "You can pay for the inventory as you sell the merchandise. My father is sick and cannot work, but we have to keep the store open."

We accepted his offer. The dairy was at Florence and 72nd Street, in the middle of Watts. We took it over a few weeks after the riots of August 1965. When the plant manager's father, a little old man, arrived to help with the inventory, we saw that his head was covered with bandages. We still didn't realize that the reason behind the generous offer was that people were afraid to run a store in Watts. We were so new and green, we didn't understand why the riots happened or what they were about. Coming from Romania, we were not prejudiced against blacks. We also didn't appreciate the difficulties and frustrations black people were facing daily or the dangerous position we were placing ourselves in. In a short time we managed to establish friendly relations with the neighbors and customers.

We worked seven days a week, sixteen hours a day. The children, now eighteen and twelve, took care of themselves. My brother Tibi, recently arrived in Los Angeles, lived and worked with us.

Around the corner from the dairy there was an elementary school. On their way to school the children would stop by the store for some sweets or fresh donuts and a small carton of milk. They would correct my pronunciation and tried to teach me English. When I spoke with their accents, my friends wondered where I had learned English.

We had the dairy for almost six months. We got to know most of the customers. Some, when they saw me carrying the heavy cases with six half-gallon bottles of milk and juices, got out from their car and took the case from me.

Afternoons were the busiest time of the day. People coming home from work stopped at the dairy to pick up milk and other groceries. One afternoon, a long line of cars was waiting to be helped. Alex and I were running back and forth, carrying cases of milk and merchandise. All of a sudden, as Alex was getting some change from the cash register, a young man approached him.

"This is a hold-up," he said.

Alex had no idea what he wanted. In a hurry to help the next customer he told him, "Can't you see I am busy? You'll have to wait your turn," and pushed him aside.

When the man pulled out a knife Alex understood. Alex looked him over and decided to take him on. Later he explained, "He was about my size, and he didn't look stronger then me. I certainly wasn't going to give him our hard-earned money." Alex grabbed the hand holding the knife and wrested it away from him. The man pulled Alex to the ground, and started to wrestle with him.

I ran to our next-door neighbor to call the police. I didn't know enough English to make the call or explain what I wanted. The neighbor, a widow who had always been very friendly to us, could tell that it was an emergency and she guessed its nature. She ran to the dairy with me with a big, long rifle dating from before World War I. The trouble was that while she was screaming at the man, she was just as likely to shoot Alex as the robber. Just then the egg delivery man arrived. Seeing Alex and the hold-up man wrestling on the floor, he rushed in to help. The hold-up man, outnumbered, ran away. We couldn't believe it. All this happened in broad daylight, with a long line of cars waiting to be helped. Perhaps the customers at the end of the line didn't realize what was happening, but those nearest to us knew and they didn't get out of their cars to help.

The egg man waited until the daily rush was over. Then he gave us advice: "I hate to lose a good customer like you. I know from my deliveries that since you took over, the sales have more than doubled. But you are newcomers to this country and you don't understand what's going on here. Did you come all the way from Romania to die here? This is not a safe place for a new immigrant to do business." After what just happened, we realized he was right. It was time to get out of the dairy business. We found someone who paid us for the inventory and took over the dairy from us, just as we had taken it over from the previous owner.

During the six months we had the dairy we saved enough money to rent a tiny place on Hollywood Boulevard. We opened a store stocked with the one dollar ties and the small selection of shirts we could afford. The store couldn't generate enough for a living, and it didn't need two people to handle it. So Alex got a job at a Hungarian place making antique furniture reproductions. He came to the store after work.

Then just as we were reaching the end of our means, bonded knit material became the rage. On the next block from our store a big sportswear store was selling some V-neck pullovers made from a bonded knit and everyone was wearing them. We bought a small used Singer home sewing machine. From a yardage store downtown, Alex bought some small remnants of bonded-knit material in different colors. Then we bought a pullover, made a pattern from it, and started making pullovers. Alex was cutting and pressing, and I was sewing all day. We hired a window trimmer to make a beautiful show window, and we put a little sign in the window saying "Custom made to order." We had reached the point of being down to just another month's rent. The sweaters changed everything. People bought two or three sweaters and pullovers made to order. Our price was lower than the price of a factory-made sweater, and they got to choose the material and style. We started making sweaters from all different kinds of double knits, all wool, and bonded knits. We had famous actors and movie-stars stopping at our little store. My English was still evolving. Once a young man was bargaining for a sweater. "If you'll give it to me for seven bucks I'll take it," he said. "Okay," I agreed, and reached to the top shelf where I had the gift boxes. When he saw me taking down seven boxes he started laughing. He explained that bucks were dollars, and he did not want boxes.

Alex was still working at the furniture place during the day. One day a customer came to order two sweaters. I could tell he was Hungarian and we started talking. From Budapest, he had emigrated to the USA in 1956 after the revolution. He was working at the Max Factor Cosmetics laboratories as the research and development supervisor for eye care products. I told him how we had just come from Romania, and how hard my husband was working at a furniture manufacturer. We became good friends and through him Alex got a job at Max Factor's Mansfield Street plant as the quality control technician for the entire plant. His workplace was five minutes from our home and about ten from the store. He started at seven o'clock in the morning. At ten he had a half-hour coffee break and drove me to the store. By that time I had finished cooking and cleaning house. During his lunch hour Alex drove downtown to buy merchandise and materials for the store. In the afternoon when he finished his work at the plant, he drove to the store to cut and press the sweaters I sewed all day. We kept the store open late, and sometimes on weekends even past midnight. At that time Hollywood Boulevard was still the promenade of the city, with movie theaters on each block and large elegant stores and expensive boutiques, famous restaurants, and nightclubs.

Alex's salary was enough for our expenses, so that all the money we made in the store could be saved. We rented a little house and bought some furniture from the shop where Alex had worked. Until then we had only a hand-me-down dining room set and mattresses. We bought a living room set, two bedroom sets, and rugs, and to complete the furnishings we looked for some pictures for the walls. We went to several art galleries, looking at the pictures which we could afford. "I will paint you nicer ones," Alex declared. He bought art supplies and started painting. Today our walls are decorated with his oil, charcoal pastel, and water color paintings.

In 1970 we sold the little store. My sister Ibi and her husband David Steinberger came to visit from Romania. Just then leather garments became the hot style. We bought some hides in small quantities of many different colors. David taught us to make all kinds of leather garments and he made us some samples. After they left, we rented a larger store on Hollywood Boulevard and furnished it as an elegant boutique for men's sportswear. We made all the fixtures by ourselves—dark brown walnut-veneered shelves and mirrored showcases. We installed a dark burgundy carpet. It looked very impressive and elegant. Alex quit his job at Max Factor; this store needed two people. We bought ready-made leather coats and a large selection of pants, dress shirts, and all kinds of men's sportswear. We also made leather garments and put a sign in the window: "Custom made leather garments."

From the very beginning the store was successful, and that made us work with more ambition. We also made stage outfits for dancing and singing groups from all over the country. We made leather and colorful crushed velvet vests. I sewed and Alex pressed and cut all day.

The demand for leather coats and garments kept increasing. The local manufacturers couldn't satisfy the demand. Alex found a partner who had imported some small quantities of materials from Austria and Turkey. Together they went to Europe and started importing large quantities of leather coats. They sold them directly to the manufacturers and distributors. Besides the wholesale imports, Alex bought the factories' showroom samples for our store. This gave us a large variety of leather garments at a very favorable price.

By 1974 we had saved enough to think of buying our own house. We started looking at houses for sale. I liked several, but we couldn't find one that would satisfy Alex.

"I will build you one," he said.

"But you don't even know how to start, and I want one now," I cried.

"I will learn, I will pay someone to teach me. It won't take that long. I have always wanted to build," he replied.

I had always trusted his instincts. We set out to find a suitable lot. That proved to be a lot more difficult than we had anticipated. Either the location wasn't right or the price was too high. One Sunday we were driving with some friends to Century City through Club View Drive when we saw a sign saying "Lot for Sale." We stopped the car to see the lot. Our friends started laughing. The lot, or what we could see of it, was a steep slope, straight up about twenty feet right from the curb. On one end of the lot there was a small wash that made it possible to climb to the top. To our surprise a huge flat lot extended in front of us. Alex looked around, walked from one end to the other, stopping at the edge of the slope. I saw him study the slope.

"I like this place," he told us, his face lighting up.

"But how are you going to climb up here?" we all asked him.

"I'll figure something out. We could build a nice house here," he said.

The price was right, and we bought the lot. The location was ideal. It was half a block south of Wilshire Boulevard, with a view of the golf club between the huge trees that surrounded it. Alex started sketching and drawing plans and solutions. We found a Hungarian architect who made the final plans and secured the necessary permits. He agreed to teach Alex, for a fee, where to buy the materials and how to hire the subcontractors.

From early morning until ten o'clock, when we went to the store, and on Sundays we worked at the construction. We did all the landscaping and installed sprinklers. Inside we built the stair railings, wall paneling, and fireplace mantle. We were trying to save as much as possible. Alex kept saying, "We have more time than money, let's use our resources wisely." We had almost finished the house when we ran out of cash. When we went to a bank for a loan, they explained that we should have applied for a construction loan before we started; banks don't make loans for a house under construction because they can't tell if there are any liens or claims against it. When the house was finished and a certificate of occupancy obtained, we could apply for a mortgage loan. Until then banks couldn't help us. We borrowed from our friends, five thousand from one, ten from another, and two or three from others, as much as they could spare. We borrowed until we had enough to finish the house. Then we took out a mortgage loan big enough to pay back all the private loans and to buy another lot. We moved into the house and furnished it. It was a beautiful house! We bought another lot, and, making sure this time to get a construction loan first, built a second house.

In the summer of 1976, we put the first house on the market and although there was an economic slowdown, the house was so beautiful that we sold it in a short time and made a large profit on it. We moved into the new house that was built on a hillside at North Bundy Drive. It was a French-style, two story-house with a circular driveway and ornamental trees in the front. Again, the two of us, Alex and I, did a lot of work inside and outside. The paneling of the family room, with its dark brown walnut plywood and ceiling with the hidden lighting, was an exhausting job. Terracing the hillside, we built raised flower beds and steps from used railroad ties, and gazebos from redwood. We planted rose bushes, shrubs, and fruit trees on the terraces. From the proceeds of the first house we paid off the construction loan. Now we owned this house free and clear from any debts, and had enough left to buy another lot.

From an ad in the papers we found a lot on the top of a hill in Bel Air. The seller was over ninety years old when we met him. He once owned the whole hilltop. Now a widower, he was living alone in his huge house. A nephew of his took care of him, bringing him necessities every week and taking him shopping occasionally. This was the last lot he was selling. It was next to his house. The lot was a downhill lot, covered with huge pine trees. We became good friends. He had lots of experience in hillside landscaping and planting. We learned many things from him. He also loaned us some money so that with the money we had, we were able to build a beautiful English Tudor-style mansion. We also managed to buy several acres of locked-in land that was adjacent to our lot at a favorable price. The land became a huge park. We built several gazebos in different shapes. We made steps from used railroad ties, cut trails on the hillsides, and built benches at lookout points and under shady trees. We built a greenhouse and planted hundreds of fruit and ornamental trees and flowering shrubs along the trails. It became a paradise on earth. Just as we finished the construction in 1979, we sold the Bundy house at a very good price. It was a sellers' market. Again, we paid off all our debts.

Alex became increasingly involved in construction and was able to spend less time in the store. So we decided to sell our store and opened a shoe store instead. Not having to work at making merchandise for the store gave Alex more time for the construction.

We were still looking for another lot to build on. One day as I was walking on the road in our neighborhood I saw a "For Sale" sign on an old little rundown house at the end of the road. I tried to convince Alex to look at it. He refused. "I am looking for a lot to build, not for an old house to remodel," he kept saying. So I went by myself out of curiosity to see the house. It was empty and in very bad shape, but as I went to the back of the lot I almost fainted, the view was so strikingly beautiful. A serene lake surrounded by mountains covered with green shrubbery lay beneath the ivy-covered slope at the end of the lot. The neighbors' houses to the left and to the right were far away and hidden by large trees. One could see only the lake, mountains, and trees—no other house or structure of any kind. I was so excited I ran home, crying, "Alex, come with me. You must see this house." Seeing me so agitated, he said, "All right I'll go see it, but I still don't want to buy a house." He changed his mind when he saw the place. We made an offer the same day, but we were late. A young couple's offer had already been accepted. We were very disappointed. I even tried to offer a profit to induce the couple to sell us the house. They wouldn't hear of it. Two years later they offered to sell us the house because they couldn't afford the payments. It was meant to be ours.

We bought it, demolished the old house, and built a house for ourselves. Although we have bought five more lots since then and built three more houses, all of them bigger and more luxurious than ours, we are not moving. The house we live in is our dream home. From the main gate to the last bush in the backyard, we built our dreams into it. And we did it all with the work of our own hands.

A glossy, coppery-green Eugenia hedge behind the wrought-iron fence hides the house from the street. A circular driveway bordered by rose trees and rose bushes behind low buxus edging and lawns with jacarandas and liquid amber trees lead up to the house. Palm trees on each side of the front porch keep sentry over the main entry. Juniper and protocarpus trees soften the wall of the white two-story colonial style house. Tall, uncut ficus hedges, huge canary pines, redwoods, and towering cypresses separate our house from those of the neighbors.

The unique beauty of our home is in the back. Each room of the house looks onto a huge deck and beyond it to

the lake and the mountains surrounding it. On the slope between the lake and deck, deer, coyotes, and squirrels hide in
the native shrubbery. There is a separate guest apartment under the deck and from its terrace, eight steps made of used
railroad ties go down to the large backyard covered with soft
green grass.

The house is big and spacious. To the left of the
two-story-tall entry are a powder room, laundry room, and
garage. To the right is the kitchen, which opens to the dining room. In the front at the right is the large living room
with a big marble fireplace and the formal dining room with
mirrored ceiling. At the front left is the spacious family room
with a fireplace and a wet bar. Beyond the family room is an
oak-paneled library with built-in bookshelves that serves as
our office. From the entry an oak staircase leads to the oval
balcony that surrounds the upstairs quarters. To its right is
the master suite. In the center is Alex's studio with skylights
and a slanted ceiling. On the other side are two guest bedrooms.

The light oak parquet floors of the entry, living room,
and dining room are covered with Persian rugs. We have Eu-
ropean furniture, Austrian crystal chandeliers, and photo-
graphs of our grandchildren, along with Alex's paintings on
the walls. It is a beautiful, warm, and spacious home. On
some Friday nights or weekends, our children and grandchildren are with us. The day before Passover Alex assembles a
long table across the dining and living room, to seat
thirty-five to forty people. Besides our children and grandchildren, my sister Ibi and her husband and my brother Tibi
and his wife and their children and grandchildren are with
us. Every year we also have a few other guests from all over
the world at the seder. Having the seder at our house is a
tradition originating from after the war in Szatmar. Then
Alex was the only one in the family to provide a seder.

Memories

At holiday times we are often overwhelmed by memories. We both like to remember how the holidays were observed in our homes. Each memory is a recaptured treasure. Last Sukkos coming home from the temple, Alex turned to me, "Rozika," (this is what he always calls me) "You know the ancient melodies the cantor and choir sang today at services? They remind me of when I was a little boy."

I remember holding my father's hand as we went to the shul. Father was in his best suit, Mother was dressed in white, my little sister and I had new clothes. Listening to the cantor and choir, I was awed by the holiness of the Kol Nidre service. I prayed so hard I am sure now that my sins were forgiven.

It is interesting how a tune can stir up memories. The melodies of Yom Tovim often bring back memories of long-forgotten events. A few years ago our cantor's daughter read the "Oz yashir" from the Torah, on a Shabbat Sirah, to a melody I haven't heard since I was in the Talmud Torah cheder of Szatmar. For me that melody is the real one, the original one. Occasionally the cantor and chorus sang the birchat cohanim *to a melody that reminds me of my first* dichening.

It was about sixty-five years ago when my father first took me to dichen under his talles. He showed me how to hold my hands and fingers and taught me the blessings. At the repetition of the musaf shemone esrah, *before the cantor started* retzei, *the cohanim removed their shoes and went to the entry. There the* leviim *poured water over our hands from a big copper cup with two handles. Two or three leviim were holding the cup, so that all of them could participate in the mitzvah. After we dried our hands we returned to our seats. Then, when the cantor chanted* vseerav, *the cohanim ascended to the platform, standing facing the ark. There were many cohanim. They filled the twenty-five- or thirty-foot-wide platform and the steps in front of the ark of the Satmare Grosse Shul. The cantor continued till* mipi Aharon uvanav. *While he chanted the last prayer in a subdued voice, we and the congregation recited quietly a short prayer assigned before the birchat cohanim. The cantor paused a minute until everything quieted down. Then he callled out loudly, "Cohanim!" Everybody replied in the proper Hebrew, "Thy holy people, as it is said." Pronouncing their own blessing in a loud voice, the cohanim covered themselves with their tallesim and with outstretched arms for blessing turned to face the congregation. The cantor, followed by the cohanim, uttered the words of the birchat cohanim, signaling with that ancient melody of the priestly blessing "ahaaaa aaa," the time necessary for the congregation to say the prayers assigned to each word of the blessing.*

I stood there under my father's talles with outstretched arms, my whole being overwhelmed with such piety and devotion as only a child can feel. Two thousand years ago the cohanim performing the service in the Holy Temple of Jerusalem could have not felt more exalted than that six- or seven-year-old boy under his father's talles.

At the end of the priestly blessing, we turned to face the ark while uttering the proper prayer and stayed there until the cantor finished the prayer sim shalom. *The congregation responded* "Umain" *and the cohanim descended and returned to their places.*

Looking Back

We have been living in Los Angeles for the past thirty years. They have been good years, productive and prosperous. America has been good to us. We have achieved more than we expected. Some people have asked us what's the secret of our success. We have no secret. Our accomplishments are the result of earnest hard work, common sense, and a little foresight. We never spent all we earned. Even when we worked for minimum wages, we saved part of our earnings. We have always devoted ourselves fully to the task at hand. Nothing ever was too hard. We always tried to find an enjoyable side in what we were doing. Above all, we were always able to work together in harmony.

We are writing this in 1995 in Bel Air, fifty years after we met. We live in the most beautiful part of the best country in the whole world. We are happy and content. We know that we were meant for each other. God has given us to each other to heal and compensate for the loss of our loved ones. Our two children are happily married, and between them they have given us five beautiful grandchildren. Our extended family may not be yet as numerous as it once was. Still, it is living proof that the Jewish people will live forever. In the last two thousand years empires, kingdoms, and nations, have risen and fallen and have disappeared without a trace. The Jewish people are still alive and will live forever.

It is Friday evening after a hot summer day. The flickering lights of the Shabbat candles make the shadows dance on the walls. Only this time it was I who lit the candles, not Mamma, and I don't light as many candles as she did. I only light two—one for the living and one for the memory of the dead. I don't turn on the lights of the chandeliers. I am sitting on the couch in the living room in the semi-darkness waiting for Alex to return from the temple. The big dinner table in the dining room is set only for two. The chala and the Kiddish wine on the white tablecloth are there waiting for the Shabbat celebration. Every time I bless the Shabbat candles I think of Mamma. If she could only see me now.

APPENDIX

Rav Yoylish Teitelbaum: A Controversial Leader

Rav Yoylish Teitelbaum was chief rabbi of Szatmar (Satu-Mare, in Romanian) from 1934. Before that he was rabbi in several communities in the Northern Carpathians and Transylvania. From 1928, after the death of Rabbi Eliezer David Grunvald, a bitter fight for the election of the new rabbi erupted within the orthodox community. The struggle lasted six years. It was concluded in 1934 with the victory of the supporters of Joel (Yoylish, as everybody called him) Teitelbaum. As a child I remember his installation. It was with great fanfare, police cordons, and a military band. As he was brought from the train station in an open horsedrawn carriage, his followers and everybody in the city were lining the streets all the way to his residence.

His uncompromising anti-Zionist stand influenced orthodox Jewry in the whole of Transylvania. He had a large group of followers who listened to him in all matters. During the Holocaust in 1944, he was saved in the rescue train arranged by Rezso Kasztner and from Bergen-Belsen he went to Erez-Israel. From there in 1947 he immigrated to the USA and settled in Williamsburg, New York. Here he established a Hasidic congregation that continued as it had in Szatmar. He was against the State of Israel and Zionism all his life; he also opposed the use of Hebrew as the spoken language and the *aliah* to Israel.

We were not the only ones for whom he caused misery. There were many other Orthodox Jews who stayed, persuaded by Rav Yoylish that it was the right thing to do. I know that he could not have known what a fateful decision that was, but I cannot find it in my heart to forgive him for it, even to this day.

Rav Yoylish survived the Holocaust and died a few years ago in New York. He was ransomed from a concentration camp by his followers. His release and that of other wealthy and influential people were arranged by Rezso Kasztner in exchange for an enormous amount of gold and dollars.

Rezso Kasztner: Was He a Collaborator?

Rezso Kasztner was a leader in the Zionist movement of Romania and later of Hungary. Kasztner was born in Cluj, Transylvania in 1906. He was a lawyer and worked as a journalist for the Hungarian-language Zionist newspaper *Uj Kelet* in Cluj. After the annexation of northern Transylvania to Hungary in 1940, Uj Kelet was closed down by the authorities.

In 1942 he moved to Budapest and joined the local Zionist movement. Soon he became the deputy chairman of the Hungarian Zionist Organization. Later he also became the head of the Zionist rescue operations. With the help of Joel Brant, a member of the Budapest relief committee who lived for many years in Germany, he succeeded in maintaining contact not only with the Hungarian leaders and opposition, but also with the German SS.

When Adolph Eichmann arrived in Budapest to apply the "Final Solution" in Hungary, Kasztner became the chief contact with Eichmann, in place of Brant, who was sent to Istanbul by the Germans to negotiate an exchange of Jews from Germany and German-occupied territories for war materials ("Blood for Goods"). Kasztner traveled several times to Germany and Switzerland to arrange the financing and rescue of close to two thousand prominent Jews from Cluj and Budapest for enormous sums of money and jewelry. Included in this group was Joel Teitelbaum, our Szatmar rabbi.

Many people felt that Kasztner was one of the real heroes of the war. Others, including Hanna Arendt, felt that he gave famous or "privileged" Jews special treatment, "which spelled death for all non-special cases."

In 1955, Judge Benjamin Halevi of the Jerusalem District Court said Kasztner "sold his soul to the devil" by collaborating with the Nazis. Halevi's decision was reversed. Judge Moshe Silberg, in his dissent from the reversal, agreed with Halevi. He felt collaborators made it easy for the Nazis to dupe their victims.

After the war, Kasztner settled in Israel. He got a government post, rejoined the *Uj Kelet* newspaper reestablished in Tel-Aviv, and was active in the Mappai party. In 1953 he was accused of collaborating with the Germans. He sued his accuser for slander. At the first trial, a lower court accepted the accusations and dismissed the slander charges. Kasztner appealed the case, which went all the way to the Supreme Court of the State of Israel. Kasztner's case became a political issue. Kasztner was shot down in the street in front of his house and died five days later. After his death, the Supreme Curt of Israel reversed the lower court's decision and cleared Kasztner's name.

Raoul Wallenberg: Unsung Hero

Raoul Wallenberg, a young Swedish diplomat, came to Budapest in 1944, and by the time he disappeared in Russian hands in 1945 he is credited with rescuing and saving the lives of 30,000 Hungarian Jews. Others have estimated that he saved as many as 100,000. Fearlessly, he defied top German Nazis like Adolph Eichman, as well as the Arrow Cross

Hungarian Nazi terrorists. Working tirelessly for long hours every day, he made himself available to those who needed his services. By risking his life daily, he provided Swedish passports and papers that made escape possible for many Jews. His efforts raised the morale and hope of Hungarian Jews whose plight had seemed hopeless.

Arrested by the Russians as a spy, he disappeared into the Gulag. The Russians apparently clouded his whereabouts in a massive cover-up. Simon Wiesenthal felt that Wallenberg deserved the Nobel Peace Prize and tried valiantly to find him, believing like many others that he was still alive many years after the war—in prison, or in a mental institution in some remote spot in Russia.

The State of Israel decreed Wallenberg a Righteous Gentile, one of its highest honors. But he was never able to collect his award in person.

Glossary

Afikoman That piece of matzo which at the beginning of the Passover night celebrations as part of the ceremony is set aside for the ending of the service

Alef-Bait Hebrew ABC's

Aliah Returning to Israel

Ausgelassent Assimilated

AVO Hungarian State Defense Detachment, or secret police

Baal tefilah Person conducting the prayers

Balebatish Proper, respected

Behoved Respected and well to do

Birchat Cohanim Hebrew for Priestly blessing

Bocher young man

Bubi Grandma

Chala Twisted white bread

Chalamoyd Intermediary holidays

Chanuka Festival of Light

Chasene Wedding ceremony

Chassids Members of a pious sect opposed to secular life, devoted to strict observance of the Jewish ritual practices

Chazan Cantor

Cheder Hebrew school

Cholent One-pot bean stew

Cholile God forbid

Chumayts Leavened bread or leavened food

Chuppa Wedding canopy

Cluj City in Romania (Kolozsvar in Hungarian)

Cohanim Priests, descendants of Aaron the high priest and his sons

Cohan A member of the priestly tribe
Corso Promenade
Csarda Inn
Dayan Rabbinical judge
Delkeli Cheese danish
Dichening The priestly blessing
Domnisoara "Miss" in Romanian
Dybbuk Evil spirit
Eil mule rachamim Mourning hymn
Eirev Symbolic fence; walled or fenced-in place
Feter Uncle
Gabela Name of ticket
Gentzen Geese
Get Divorce
Got in himmel God in heaven
Griveleh Roasted skin
Hora Folk dance
Himmel Heaven
Interfirers Persons who lead the bride under the chuppa
Ken ayen'hore Let not an evil eye see you
Kiddish Blessing on the wine
Kol Nidrei The introductory prayer on Yom Kippur night
Korut Circular avenue
Krishme Prayer at bedtime
Kulak Large landowners; considered exploiters of the people
Leviim Levites; members of the Levi tribe
Machzur Holiday prayer book
Makheteyneste Mother-in-law
Mashgiach Supervisor of ritual correctness
Matzo Unleavened bread eaten at Passover
Mazel tov Good luck
Mezuzah A parchment with a blessing sat on the door post
Mikve Jewish public bathhouse
Mime Aunt
Mipi Aharon uvanav From the mouth of Aaron and his sons

Mitzvah Good deed, meritorious deed

Motzi Blessing for bread

Nadin Dowry

Nor asoyfil Is this all

Nyilas Party Arrow Cross Party; Hungarian Nazi party

Oz yashir A prayer; song of Moses at the Red Sea

Parnusi Livelihood

Pengo Hungarian currency

Pesach Passover

Peyes Ear locks

Purim Festival for celebrating and rejoicing the triumph of Queen Esther and her Uncle Mordechai over Haman, the villain

Purim spiel Purim play

Rav, Reb Abbreviation for Rabbi

Rebe Teacher

Rebetzen Rabbi's wife

Retzei Prayer starting with "Be gracious"

Richu Devil

Rosh Bet Din Chief of the ritual court

Rosh Hashanah New Year

Sachrit and Musav Shmoneh Esrah The standing prayers for Saturday morning

Satmare Grosse Shul The big temple of Szatmar

Schimbas A volunteer cavalry cadet in the old Romanian army

Schnorrers Professional beggars

Securitate Romanian state security police

Seder Passover night celebration and dinner

Sedre The weekly Torah portion

Shabbat Shirah Sabbath of the song of Moses

Shadchen Marriage broker

Shalech mones Gifts of food at Purim

Shaytl Wig

Shefele My little lamb

Shevuos Spring festival; Feast of Weeks

Shidech Match for marriage

Shiva To "sit shiva" is to mourn a family member by sitting on the floor for seven days after the death

Shoychet Ritual slaughterer

Shtramli A fur hat made from thirteen sable tails

Shul Temple

Siderles Everyday prayer books

Sim shalom Prayer starting with "Grant peace"

Statescu temple Reform temple (corruption of "Status quo")

Sukkah Symbolic booth or hut

Sukkos Fall holiday, Festival of the Booths

Tachrichem Burial dress

Taig essen To eat with a different family each day of the week

Talles Prayer shawl

Talmud Torah Name of a Hebrew school

Thilem Psalms

Tovarasul Comrade

Treyfe foods prohibited by Jewish dietary laws

Tsores Misery, trouble

Tsu fis un tsu kopens Head to feet

Tzedaka Alms

Umain Amen

Vayshet Gullet

Vice Assistant Superintendent in Hungarian

Vseerav Prayer starting with "May our prayers be acceptable"

Waber-shul Women's section in the temple

Yom Kippur High holiday of repentance

Yom Tovim Holidays

Zaydi Grandpa

Zmirot After-meal prayers and songs

Bibliography

The Politics of Genocide, Vols. I and II, by Randoulph I. Braham; Columbia University Press, 1981.

Justice in Jerusalem, by Gideon Hausner; Waldon Press, 1077.

Righteous Gentile, by John Bierman; The Viking Press, 1981.

Wallenberg: Missing Hero, by Kati Marton; Random House, 1982.

The War Against the Jews, by Luci S. Dawidowitz; Holt, Reinhart, Winston, 1975.

Encyclopaedia Judaica, Keter Publishing House.